The Chatelaine of Vergi

Alice Kempwelch

BIBLIOLIFE

Copyright © BiblioLife, LLC

BiblioLife Reproduction Series: Our goal at BiblioLife is to help readers, educators and researchers by bringing back in print hard-to-find original publications at a reasonable price and, at the same time, preserve the legacy of literary history. The following book represents an authentic reproduction of the text as printed by the original publisher and may contain prior copyright references. While we have attempted to accurately maintain the integrity of the original work(s), from time to time there are problems with the original book scan that may result in minor errors in the reproduction, including imperfections such as missing and blurred pages, poor pictures, markings and other reproduction issues beyond our control. Because this work is culturally important, we have made it available as a part of our commitment to protecting, preserving and promoting the world's literature.

All of our books are in the "public domain" and some are derived from Open Source projects dedicated to digitizing historic literature. We believe that when we undertake the difficult task of re-creating them as attractive, readable and affordable books, we further the mutual goal of sharing these works with a larger audience. A portion of BiblioLife profits go back to Open Source projects in the form of a donation to the groups that do this important work around the world. If you would like to make a donation to these worthy Open Source projects, or would just like to get more information about these important initiatives, please visit www.bibliolife.com/opensource.

THE CHATELAINE OF VERGI: A ROMANCE OF THE XIIITH CENTURY: TRANSLATED BY ALICE KEMP-WELCH: THE FRENCH TEXT FROM THE EDITION RAYNAUD: INTRODUCTION BY BRANDIN, PH.D.

CHATTO & WINDUS : PUBLISHERS
LONDON : 1909

"VOILÀ, MESDAMES, L'HISTOIRE QUE VOUS M'AVEZ PRIÉE DE VOUS RACOMPTER, QUE JE CONGNOIS BIEN À VOZ ŒILS N'AVOIR ÉTÉ ENTENDUE SANS COMPASSION."

—MARGUERITE DE NAVARRE.

All rights reserved

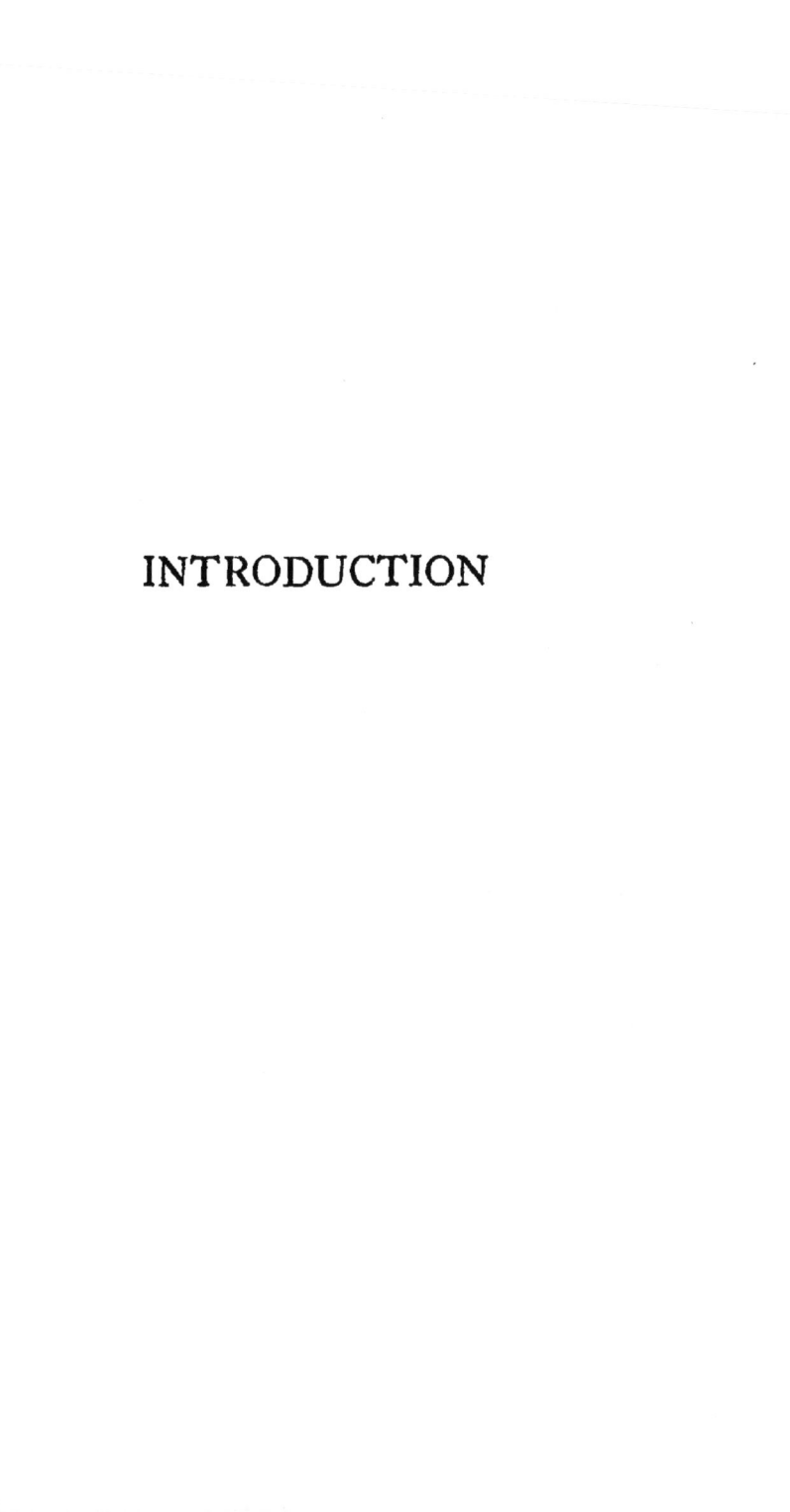

INTRODUCTION

Dg

INTRODUCTION

AT the Court of the Dukes of Burgundy, as well as at that of the Count of Flanders, and amongst the *entourage* of Queen Margaret of Navarre, the dainty story of the Chatelaine of Vergi caused many tears to be shed. It made the hearts of many great lords and ladies beat, and excited the pity of many a poet. Touching allusions to the heroine of the story have been made by various illustrious writers. Froissart, for example, guided by Dame Pleasance and Dame Esperance into the garden of King Love, saw her there with Helen, Genievre, Isoud, Hero, Polyxena, Dame Equo, and Medea, and he ranks her love with the sad loves of

THE CHATELAINE OF VERGI

Tristran and Isoud, and of the Lady of Fayel and the Chatelain of Couci.

Coming to us thus, escorted by long centuries of tears and admiration, the Lady of Vergi does not need a lengthy introduction. Her tragic story appears here in its original form, and her sublime love will give pleasure to-day for the self-same reasons which, in the time of Philip le Bel and Edward I., held the noble ladies of Burgundy and Flanders under its spell. All that can be said is that, after the lapse of six centuries, some of the features of the story may appear somewhat antiquated, and that, perchance, it may surprise some fair reader, possessed of only a dim notion of the code of love which prevailed in the glorious age of chivalry to learn that the mere knowledge that her secret had been betrayed by her lover could, at the end of the thirteenth century, cause the death of a noble lady. Even with this wrinkle on its brow, and with others which a careful search may disclose, this little romance bears gaily its well-nigh six hundred and fifty years. The absence of the conventional and the traditional, the depth and variety of the psychological analysis, the naïveté of the moral, the unexpectedness of the philosophical ideas—these are the causes of its eternal youth. The colours in which the author has painted the various characters in the story, and the sentiments which he has attributed to them, retain, and will ever retain, their original freshness. One reads and re-reads the pages where he describes the base jealousy of the Duchess; her utilitarian conception of the love by which she tries to allure the brave Knight; her influence over her weak husband, unable to sleep as soon as she has persuaded him that one of his vassals has threatened his honour, and equally unable to keep a secret when his wife turns her back

6   THE CHATELAINE OF VERGI

upon him in bed; those, again, where both the cleverness and the artlessness of the Chatelaine stand out; those where, in her pathetic agony, she pours forth bitter regrets, which soon give place to a sad resignation, to end in a last thought of pardon for him whose treachery has killed her; those where the character of the Knight is portrayed by his uprightness and by his want of tact, as well as by his hesitation between the loss of his mistress and that of his honour; and those, finally, where so openly, so innocently, and so intelligently, the little dumb messenger carries, on his four paws, the hopes of the two lovers.

Is this little romance as true to fact as it is realistic? M. Gaston Raynaud tells us in the following words what *he* feels on this point, when he says: "The poet, writing after the event, has dramatised the story of a great scandal at the Court of Burgundy between 1267 and

INTRODUCTION

1272, a scandal in which Hugo IV., Beatrice of Champagne, and Laura of Lorraine certainly played a part" (*Romania*, xxi. p. 153). This suggestion is interesting, but as the romance was written about the year 1280, according to M. Gaston Paris (see his *Littérature française du moyen âge*, second edition, p. 253), or between 1282 and 1288 in the opinion of M. Raynaud, the author must have been a contemporary of the personages alluded to, and thus it is hardly conceivable that he should have ventured to take such liberties with current events as he must have done if he was recording the scandal alluded to. He must have known, in common with every one else in Burgundy at the time, that Hugo IV. died in 1272 at St. James of Compostella, and yet he tells us that "he went on a crusade beyond the sea, *from whence he returned not*, for there he became a Templar."

Still less comprehensible is it that he should

8 THE CHATELAINE OF VERGI

have ventured to place the date of Laura of Lorraine's death at least ten years earlier than the actual date, which must necessarily have been *after* 1281, as in that year, as we learn from Du Chesne's *Histoire de la Maison de Vergy*, she did homage to Otho, Count of Burgundy, on the Tuesday after the Feast of St. Bartholomew, for her dower of the Seignory of St. Autrey. And last of all, it is inconceivable that he should have represented Hugo IV. as having killed Beatrice of Champagne whose death only occurred in 1295, *i.e.* twenty-three years after Hugo IV. had quitted this world, and thirteen years (or, if we admit the *terminus ad quem* given by M. Raynaud, possibly only seven years) after the story was written. These strong objections against the value of this historical estimate of the story lead us to suppose that the author, who, as we gather from a few peculiarities of the dialect to which

INTRODUCTION

his work belongs, was a Burgundian, was writing for a Burgundian public, and was naturally induced to choose the names of Vergi and Burgundy on account of the personal interest which he himself took in his, and which he thought his countrymen would take in their, own province, as well as on account of the pleasure it would give to all Burgundians to find an interesting story connected with scenes familiar to them.

The poem has come down to us in eight MSS. of the thirteenth and fourteenth centuries, and seven of the fifteenth and sixteenth centuries. Ten of these are in Paris. They are all in the Bibliothèque Nationale, and bear the following numbers:—375 (written in 1288), 780 (end of the fifteenth century), 837 (end of the thirteenth century), 1555 (fourteenth century), 2136 (fourteenth century), and 2236 (fifteenth century), 4531 (beginning of the fourteenth century), 15219 (sixteenth century), 25545 (thirteenth century), and Moreau 1719 (an eighteenth-century copy of a MS. of the end of the thirteenth or beginning of the fourteenth century).

The Municipal Library at Valenciennes possesses one MS., No. 398 (fifteenth century), and there is one in the Royal Library at Berlin, Hamilton 257 (end of the thirteenth century), one in the Library at Hamburg (middle of the fifteenth century), and one in the Bodleian Library, 445 (second half of the fifteenth century). It is difficult to classify these MSS. strictly, and hitherto it has only been possible satisfactorily to edit the *Chatelaine of Vergi* from the earliest ones.

The first edition is the result of the labours of Méon in 1808, and appeared in vol. iv. of *Fabliaux et Contes*, pp. 296 to 326. It only takes into account the MSS. 375, 837, and 25545.

INTRODUCTION

The second edition appeared in 1892, in vol. xxi. of the *Romania*. M. Gaston Raynaud, to establish his text, made use of the thirteenth and fourteenth century MSS. only. None of these MSS. are derived immediately from the original text. They all contain, indeed, one error which seems to throw a new light upon their common origin. They all have, in verse 393, "le chevalier," instead of "le chienet." This shows that they must be referred back to some earlier MS., where the abbreviation *ch'* had been already wrongly interpreted as signifying what it usually does, *Chevalier*, whereas in this instance it ought to have received an entirely different rendering, namely *Chienet*.

In addition to an ably edited text, M. Raynaud's edition contains an introduction which gives the most complete information about the early MSS., the transcripts, and the popularity of this romance, and one cannot do better than

12 THE CHATELAINE OF VERGI

refer the reader to it. Above all, he will find portrayed there, by a master-hand, the fate that befell this story from the end of the thirteenth century onwards. He will see how the Lady of Vergi became, as early as the fourteenth century, the Lady of Vergier, and how she was confounded, at the end of the eighteenth century, with the heroine of a romance which enjoyed the greatest success in the Middle Ages—the *Chatelain of Couci*. The success of the *Chatelaine of Vergi* was considerable. It was copied and translated in France, and in other places abroad. The poem was so much in vogue, that it comes down to us, as mentioned already, in as many as fifteen MSS.

In the fourteenth century a Netherlandish edition, in verse, appeared, printed straight from the original French, says M. Raynaud, and this became the source of a popular version printed for the first time at Antwerp about 1550,

INTRODUCTION

and reprinted at Amsterdam in the seventeenth century. In France some unknown writer revived it, about 1540, in a new form, under the title of *Livre d'amours du chevalier et de la dame chastellaine du Vergier comprenant l'estat de leur amour et comment elle fut continuèe jusques à la mort.*

Marguerite of Navarre hardly did more than translate it into prose in the seventieth tale, seventh day of the *Heptameron*. Bandello reproduced, in part iv. of his *Novelle*, and almost without change, Marguerite of Navarre's version. François de Belleforest retranslated into French Bandello's story, and it forms No. 84 of his *Histoires tragiques de Bandello*. In the eighteenth century it became a work of pure fiction, from the pen of M. de Vignacourt, in *La Comtesse de Vergi, nouvelle historique, galante et tragique*, and from that of an anonymous writer who published in 1766 *La Comtesse de Vergi et Raoul de*

14 THE CHATELAINE OF VERGI

Couci, époux et amans fidèles, histoires véritable, galante et tragique.

Paper and parchment did not suffice to tell the story of the Chatelaine of Vergi; ivory also was used to perpetuate its memory. An ivory casket of the fourteenth century, now in Case F in the Mediæval Room in the British Museum, represents the various episodes of the story with great accuracy. It is from this casket that the illustrations accompanying this translation have been taken. The finish of detail, and the naïveté and variety of the figures, are remarkable, as is also the harmonious grouping of the individuals represented. This casket differs very little from another one in the Louvre (noticed in M. Émile Molinier's *Catalogue du Musée du Louvre*), which also has great artistic value, and likewise dates from the fourteenth century. The only difference between the two is to be found in the addition of a scene which is only represented on the Louvre casket, the eighteenth compartment of which shows the Duke, after beheading the Duchess with his sword, kneeling before an ecclesiastic, by whom he is being blessed and presented with a cross.

There are also various fragments of caskets in existence which represent the same subject (see *Le Catalogue de l'Exposition retrospective de l'art français au Trocadéro, in* 1889, p. 18, Nos. 122 and 123), and which prove the favour in which the poem was held.

Our personal researches in the "Salle des estampes" of the Bibliothèque Nationale, and in several other places, have not put us on the track of any other documents inspired by the *Chatelaine of Vergi*. There must, however, be others. On tapestries particularly this legend must often have been represented, and we hope that some reader, fond of archæological research, will be induced to follow up the search in other directions, and not be discouraged by the failure of our own efforts.

In conclusion, our sincerest thanks are due to all those who have been so good as to give us their aid : to the late M. Gaston Paris, to Messrs. Picot and Paul Meyer, and above all to M. Gaston Raynaud, who, with his habitual courtesy, has given permission for the reproduction of the text of the poem which he published in the *Romania*, and in which reproduction only a few modifications of his text have been introduced, the only one of any importance being the one in verse 393 alluded to above.

L. BRANDIN.

TRANSLATION

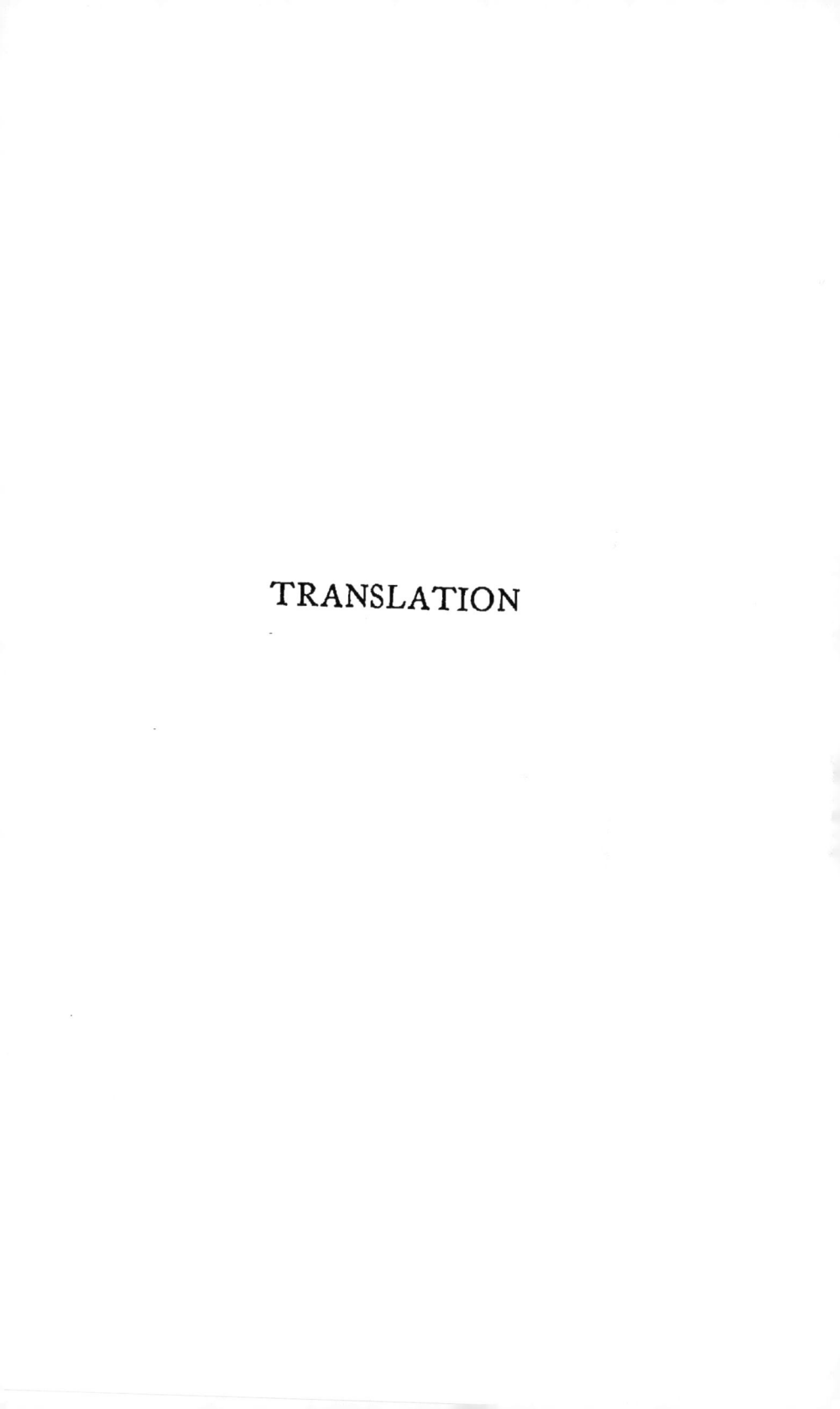

THE CHATELAINE OF VERGI

SOME there are who make pretence to be loyal, and so truly to keep secret that which is confided to them, that in the end trust is put in them. But when it happens that any one has been so indiscreet as to let them know of his love and of his doings, forthwith they noise it abroad, and make merry over it. And thus it comes to pass that he who has made known the secret, loses all delight, since the greater the love between true lovers, the more grieved are they when either thinks that that which should have been kept secret, has been made known by the other. And ofttimes does such mischief come of it, that their love must needs end in great sorrow and shame, as it chanced in Burgundy to a valiant and brave Knight, and to the Lady of Vergi, whom the Knight loved so well, that the Lady gave him her love on this condition, that whensoever he should discover unto another their love, on that day would he lose her love, and the gift which she had made to him of herself. And to enjoy their love, they devised for the Knight to come alway into an orchard when she should appoint, and in nowise to stir from one corner of it until he had seen a little dog cross the orchard. Then without tarrying might he come to her chamber, and know well that he would find his lady alone.

Thus, unknown to any, did their sweet and secret love longwhile dure. The knight was handsome and brave, and by reason of his valour he was in favour with the Duke who ruled Burgundy. And ofttimes did he go to the Court, and so oft went he, that the Duchess conceived a love for him, and made such show of her love, that had not his heart been elsewhere, readily would he indeed have perceived from her look that she loved him. But no response did the Knight make to all her tender glances, nor did he perceive that she loved him, and because of this she was sore vexed, and, on a day, thus spake she to him: "Sire, you are handsome and brave, so say all, God be thanked, and thus you have rightly deserved to have for friend one of so high rank that honour and advantage may come to you of it. How well would such a friend become you!"

"My lady," said he, "never have I yet given thought to this."

"By my faith," said she, "meseemeth a long waiting may be harmful to you. So I counsel you that you may bear yourself friendly in a certain high place if that you would be well loved there."

And he made answer: "By my faith, my lady, I know not wherefore you speak thus, or the purport of your words, neither am I Duke or Count to have right to love in so high a place, and, moreover, in nowise could I win the love of so sovereign a lady even if I made great endeavour thereto."

"You have, perchance," said she. "There has happened many a greater marvel, and the like may happen again. Tell me if you do not now know that I have given you my love, I who am a lady of high degree."

And forthwith the Knight made answer: "My lady, I know it not, but I would desire to possess your love in a right and honourable way. But may God preserve me from that love between you and me which would bring shame to my lord, for by no means would I in anywise undertake aught so dishonourable as to cause base and disloyal wrong to my rightful and liege lord."

"For shame!" said she, wrathful. "And who, Sir Knave, asked this of you?"

"Ah, my lady," said he, "I well understand, thank God, but I have said enough."

And no more did she hold speech with him, but in her heart she was very wroth and much cast down, and she thought within herself that if she could, certes she would be avenged of him, for she was much an-angered. And that night, as she lay beside the Duke, she began to sigh, and then to weep. And forthwith the Duke asked of her what ailed her, and bade her straightway tell him. Then said she: "Truly it greatly grieves me that a noble lord knows not who is faithful to him, and who is not, and, moreover, bestows goodwill and honour on those who are traitors to him, though he perceives it not."

"By my faith, lady," said the Duke, "I know not wherefore you speak thus, but of this I am quit, for by no means would I wittingly nourish a traitor."

"Then hate this one," said she (and she named unto him the Knight), "who has ceased not the whole day long to pray me for my love. Longtime, said he, had he thought on this, but ne'er had he dared utter it. And I was resolved, good sire, to make it known unto you, for it may be true that he has longwhiles thought on this, for never have we heard tell that he loves another. So I pray you, in requital, to protect your honour, since you know this to be right."

And the Duke, to whom this seemed very grievous, made answer: "This shall I settle, and that, I bethink me, right soon."

And that night the Duke was ill at ease, and had no sleep because of the Knight, whom he loved, since he believed that he had done him such wrong as to have justly forfeited his love.

And all that night he lay awake. And on the morrow he arose early, and sent for him whom his wife had caused him to hate, albeit he had done no wrong. And as soon as they were alone together he said : "Truly is it distressful to think that you are so brave and so handsome, and yet without loyalty. In this have you much deceived me, for longwhile have I thought you faithful and loyal, at least to me, for I have loved you. I know not how so traitorous a thought could have come to you as to ask of the Duchess her love. Such treachery have you committed, that naught more villainous could be conceived. Quit my territory forthwith, for certes I banish you from it, and wholly forbid and deny it unto you. Never enter it more, and know well that if ever I chance to catch you in it, I will have you hanged."

And when the Knight heard this, he was filled with anger and vexation, so that he trembled in every limb when he thought on his Love, of whom he knew that he could have no joy if that he could not go to and fro, and return to the country whence the Duke would banish him; and great dole made he also that the Duke should unjustly hold him for a disloyal traitor. And he was in such sore trouble, that he thought of himself as dead and as betrayed. "Sire," said he, "for God's sake never believe, or even think, that I have ever been so daring. Certes, never have I for a single day or a single hour thought on that with the which you so wrongfully charge me. Whosoever has told this unto you, has done evil."

"Naught will it avail you to deny it," said the Duke. "Without doubt it is the truth. The lady herself has made known to me the way in which, like a vile traitor, you have besought her, and perchance you have said that to her of the which she keeps silence."

And the Knight, sore grieved, made answer: "My lady has said what it pleases her, and it avails me not to gainsay her. Naught that I may say can profit me, nor is there aught that I can do by the which I may be believed that this has never happened."

"On my soul that is so," said the Duke, who thought on his wife, for verily he felt well assured that she had said truly that never had one heard tell that the Knight loved another. Then said he to the Knight: "If you will swear to me on your fealty that you will truly make answer to me in that which I shall ask of you, by your words I shall know of a certainty whether or no you have done that of the which I have suspicion against you."

And the Knight, who desired greatly to turn away his lord from the undeserved anger which he bare him, and who feared such loss as to quit the country where was the one who gave him most joy, replied that without demur he would do as the Duke had said, for he thought not but on that which disquieted the Duke, and in nowise did he bethink him that the Duke would question him touching any other matter. And thus he took his oath, and the Duke accepted his plighted word.

And thereupon the Duke said to him: "Know in very truth that I have so loved you heretofore with all my heart, that I could in nowise believe of you such baseness or such villany as the Duchess has told unto me, and not a whit should I hold it as true if this did not make me believe it, and put me in sore doubt, when I observe your demeanour and countenance, and other things beside, by the which it can be known full well that you love some one, whoever it may be; and as, moreover, it is not known to any one the maiden or the lady whom you love, I bethink me that it may be my wife,

THE CHATELAINE OF VERGI

who has told to me that you have besought her love. Thus I cannot be persuaded by aught that any one may say that this is not so, unless you make known to me that you so love another, that you leave me altogether without doubt that I know the whole truth. And if this you will not do, then forthwith shall you depart out of my territory as a perjured man."

And the Knight wist not what to do, for he was put to so difficult a choice, that either way he would lose. If he spake the simple truth, the which he must needs do without he perjured himself, he held himself as lost, for if he did so great wrong as to break the condition which he had with his lady and his love, of a surety he would lose her were she to discover it, and if he told not the truth to the Duke, then would he be a perjured man, and a breaker of his faith, and he would lose both his country and his Love. But naught would he trouble about his country if that he kept his Love, whom above all he feared to lose.

And when he had called to mind the great joy and the solace that he had had in her embrace, he thought thus unto himself, that if he did her any hurt, and if by his wrongdoing he lost her, since he could not take her with him, how could he dure without her? It was with him as with the Chatelain of Couci, who having in remembrance only his Love, said in a verse of one of his songs :—

> Pardie, Love, cruel is the remembrance
> Now of that sweet solace and company
> And joy mine eyes had in the countenance
> Of her who was both fellow and friend to me.
>
> When I think on her simple courtesy,
> And the sweet words that she was wont to say,
> How can my heart endure in my body?
> Certes, it is an evil thing to stay.

And in such anguish was the Knight, that

THE CHATELAINE OF VERGI

he wot not whether to make known the truth, or to lie and leave the country.

And whilst he thus pondered, and knew not the which would be the better for him, hot tears came into his eyes, and ran down his cheeks, because of the anguish which possessed him, so that his face was quite wet. And the Duke was heavy at heart, for he thought within himself that something there was that the Knight dared not discover unto him. And he said, in haste to the Knight: "I see well that you do not trust in me as much as you should. Bethink you that if you privily tell me your secret, I shall make it known unto any one? Certes, before doing this, I would let my teeth be pulled out one by one."

"Ah!" made answer the Knight, "God's mercy on me, sire, I wot not what I should say or what will happen to me, but rather would I die than lose her whom I should lose if I told unto you the truth, and she came to know that, whilst I yet lived, I had confessed it."

Then said the Duke: "I swear to you on my body, and on my soul, and on the love and faith that I owe to you in return for your homage, that in all my life it shall neither be told by me to any living creature, nor shall allusion of any kind be made thereto."

And the Knight, weeping, said to him: "Sire, then will I tell it to you. I love your niece of Vergi, and she loves me, as much as is possible."

"Tell me now, if you would be believed," said the Duke. "Knows no one save you two of this?"

And the Knight answered him, "Not a living creature."

Then said the Duke: "This can never be! In what manner, then, do you come to her, and how know you the place and the time?"

"By my faith, sire," said he, "that will I tell you forthwith, without concealing aught, since you know thus much of our affair." And then he recounted unto him all his goings to and fro, and the prior compact, and the behaviour of the little dog.

Then said the Duke: "I demand of you your consent that, at your next tryst, I be your companion, and go with you to this place, for I would know without delay that all is so, and my niece will know naught of it."

"Sire," said the Knight, "willingly do I consent to this provided it will not give you trouble or weary you, and know forsooth that I go this very night."

And the Duke said that he would go, and that in nowise would it weary him, but would be to him a solace and a pleasure. And together they devised where they could fitly meet.

And as soon as it was nightfall, as the place

where the Duke's niece dwelt was nigh at hand, they betook them thither until they were come to the garden, and there the Duke waited not long ere he saw his niece's little dog come to the corner of the orchard, where it found the Knight, who made much ado over it. And the Knight at once left the Duke, and went his way. And the Duke followed after him close to the chamber, and there remained quite still. And he concealed himself as he best could. And by a lofty and spreading tree, well fitted to screen him, he was hidden as by a shield. And from there he saw the little dog enter the chamber, and then saw his niece come forth and go towards the Knight in the meadow, and he saw and heard the greeting she gave him by joyfully calling to him, and waving her hand. And she clasped him in her fair arms, and kissed him more than an hundred times ere they held converse together. And the Knight kissed her oft, and clasped her in his arms and said to her: "My lady, my love, my friend, my heart, my mistress, my hope, and all that I love, know that I have greatly hungered to be with you, even as I am now, since last I saw you."

And she answered him: "My sweet lord and friend, and my dear love, never has a day or an hour passed that I have not wearied of the delay. But now naught troubles me, for I have by me all that I desire as you are well and content. May you be very happy!"

And the Knight said: "May you be welcome!"

And the Duke, who was crouching down quite close to them at the door, heard all, and so well were the voice and the manner of his niece known to him, that no longer was he in doubt, and he determined that that which the Duchess had told unto him was false, and greatly was he pleased, for now he saw well that the Knight had wronged him not in such manner as he had had suspicion of him.

And there remained he all the night, whilst the Lady and the Knight were in the chamber in a bed, and, without sleeping, had such happiness and solace one of another, that it is but fitting that no one should speak of it, or give heed to it, who expects not to have that joy which love gives for reward to those who love truly; for he who expects not such joy, naught does he understand when he hears tell of it, since he has not his heart set towards love, for none can in anywise know of what worth is such joy if love has not made it known to him. And this happiness comes by no means to all, for it is a joy without bitterness, as well as a solace and a delight. But to the lover it seems to last but a short while, and that it will never dure long enough. And so pleasing to him is the life he leads, that he would that

THE CHATELAINE OF VERGI

the night were a week, and that the week were a month, and the month a year, and the year three years, and three years twenty, and twenty years an hundred. And when it is ended, he would that the night should come over again before the day break.

In suchwise pondered he whom the Duke awaited. But it behoved him to depart ere break of day, and his Love came with him to the door. And as they took leave one of another, the Duke saw kisses given, and kisses returned, and he heard deep sighs and weeping as they bade each other farewell. Then many tears were shed, and the Duke heard them name the time when they should again meet there. Thus did the Knight depart, and the lady closed the door. But as long as she could see him, she followed him with her beautiful eyes, since naught beside could she do.

And when the Duke saw that the door was

closed, he forthwith went his way until he was come up with the Knight, who complained unto himself that too shortwhile for him had the night dured. And she from whom he had parted thought and spake in like manner, for it seemed to her that the night had been too short for her delight, and she welcomed not the dawn.

Thus thought and spake the Knight as the Duke came up with him and embraced him, and made much ado over him. Then said the Duke to him: "I swear to you that ever henceforth I shall love you, and never again shall I harry you, for all that you have told unto me is true, and you have not lied by one word unto me."

"Sire," said the Knight, "I pray you thanks. But by the grace of God, I demand and pray of you that you disclose not this secret, else shall I lose my Love, and all joy and comfort, and without doubt I shall die if I know that another than you have knowledge of it."

"Speak not of it," said the Duke, "and know that it will be so well kept secret, that no word of it shall ever be uttered by me."

And thus communing, they came to the place whence they had set out. And that day, when they were met to eat, the Duke looked more kindly at the Knight than ever before, and indeed so filled with anger and mortification at this was the Duchess, that she arose from the table, and feigned to be overcome of sickness, and she went to lay her down on her bed, where she had little delight. And the Duke, when he had well feasted, and washed, straightway went to her, and made her to sit up on her bed, and commanded that none save himself should remain in the chamber. And forthwith it was done as he commanded.

And the Duke at once asked of her how this

sickness had come to her, and what ailed her. And she made answer: "My God! never until now, when I sat me down to eat, did I suspect that you had not in you more of sense and reason than I perceived when you treated as more dear to you than ever, him who I have told you has sought to shame and humiliate me; and when I saw that you looked on him more kindly even than afore, such great sorrow and anger took possession of me, that no longer could I stay."

"Ah, sweet friend!" said the Duke, "know that never shall I believe, either of you or any other, that ever by any chance has that happened of the which you have told me, for I wot well that he is wholly quit of it, and that he never took thought to do this. Thus much have I learnt of his affair. So inquire not further of me concerning this."

And thereupon the Duke left her, and she

remained very pensive, for never a day that she lived would she have an hour's peace until she had learnt more of that of the which the Duke had forbidden her to question him; and now no prohibition could restrain her, for a ruse suggested itself unto her by the which she could of a certainty know all if she but waited patiently until the night, when she had the Duke in her embrace. Well knew she that without doubt such solace would win her her desire better than aught else. Therefore for this she waited, and when the Duke was come to bed, she withdrew to one side. And she made pretence that it gave her no joy that the Duke should be beside her, for well knew she that to make semblance of anger was the way to make her husband yield. Therefore thus did she remain, that she might the better make the Duke believe that she was much an-angered. And as soon as he had kissed her, she said: "Very false and treacherous and disloyal are you, who make show of love for me, and yet have never loved me for a single day. Longwhile have I been so foolish as to believe you when you have oft-times told me that you loved me with a loyal heart; but now I well see that in this I have been deceived."

And the Duke said: "In what manner?"

"By my faith," said she, filled with evil longing, "already have you enjoined that I adventure not to make inquiry concerning that which you are now so well acquainted with."

"In God's name, of what are you thinking?"

"Of that which that man has related unto you," said she, "and the lies and the deceits which he has made you give heed to and to believe. But no desire have I to know of this for of little worth do I deem it to love you with a loyal heart; for whether it was for good or ill, never did I see or hear aught which I did not

THE CHATELAINE OF VERGI 43

make known to you at once. And now I see that, of your grace, you hide from me your own thoughts. Therefore know, without doubt, that never more shall I have such trust in you, or such love of you, as I have had heretofore."

Then began the Duchess to weep and to sigh, and she made as much ado as she could. And such pity had the Duke for her, that he said to her: "My sweet friend, by no means can I endure your anger or your wrath; but know that I cannot tell you that which you desire without committing too great villainy."

And at once she made answer: "Sire, if you tell it not to me, then from this I see well that apparently you trust me not to keep your secret. And know that I much marvel at this, for never has any secret, either great or small, that you have told me, been made known by me, and

I tell you in good faith that never, whiles I live, will this come to pass."

And when she had thus spoken, she again wept. And the Duke embraced and kissed her, and so ill at ease was his mind, that no longer could he resist his desire to discover unto her the secret. Wherefore he said to her: "By my soul, dear lady, I know not what to do, for so great trust have I in you, that I believe me it is not right to hide from you aught that I have knowledge of; but greatly do I fear that you will repeat it. Know then, and I now forewarn you, that if you betray me, you shall die for it."

And she said: "Wholly do I agree to this. It cannot be that I should do you any wrong."

Then he who loved her, for that he believed her, and thought within himself that she spake truly unto him, related unto her all the story of his niece, even as he had learnt it from the

Knight, and how that he was in a corner of the orchard where only they two were, when the little dog came to them. And he told her truly of her coming out, and of their going in together, and kept back from her naught of that which he had seen and heard. And when the Duchess heard that the Knight loved one of lower rank, and for this had rejected her, she seemed to herself as dead and despised, but never did she let this be seen, but agreed, and made promise to the Duke, to keep the matter secret, and that if it should be made known by her, then might he hang her up to a branch.

And she longed greatly to have speech with her whom she hated from that hour when she learnt that she was the Love of him who had brought on her both shame and grief, because he would not, so she thought, be her own Love. And she firmly resolved that if at any time, or in any place, she saw the Duke speak with his niece, at once would she herself speak with her, and would not keep back that in which there would be felony. But never did this chance until the time of Pentecost was come at the first feast when the Duke held plenary Court, to the which he sent to summon all the ladies of the land, and, before all, his niece, who was chatelaine of Vergi.

And as soon as the Duchess saw her, immediately all her blood was stirred within her, since she hated her more than all else in the world. But she knew how to hide her feelings, and welcomed her more graciously than ever she had done aforetime. But very greatly did she long to speak of that which so much an-angered her, and the delay grieved her much. And on the day of Pentecost, when the tables were removed, the Duchess led the ladies aside to her chamber to deck them for to appear quaintly dressed at the carole. Then the Duchess, who

THE CHATELAINE OF VERGI

perceived her opportunity, could not restrain herself, and said, as though in a jest: "Chatelaine, make you very quaint, for you have as acquaintance a handsome and brave lover."

And she made answer simply: "Of a truth, my lady, I know not what acquaintance you have in mind, but I desire not to have for lover any one who may not be in all things to mine own honour, and to that of my lord."

"Right well do I grant this," said the Duchess, "but you are a clever mistress to have learned how to train the little dog."

And the ladies heard what was said, but knew not to what it referred. And then they went with the Duchess to the caroles which were going on.

And the Chatelaine remained behind. And her heart was filled with anguish, and she paled and wholly changed colour. And she withdrew into an inner chamber where lay a handmaider at the foot of the bed, though she could not see her. And the Chatelaine, grieving sorely, sank down on to the bed, and made complaint and lamentation unto herself, and said : " Alas, my God, have pity on me! How comes it that I have heard my lady reproach me in that I have made use of my little dog? That, as I well know, she can have learned from no one save from him whom I loved, and who has betrayed me. Never could he have told it unto her were it not that they have had close acquaintance, and that, since that he has betrayed me, he doubtless loves her more than he does me! Well do I now perceive that he loves me not at all since he fails in his oath to me. Dear God! I loved him as much as any one could love another, and not an hour of the day or of the night could I think of any other. For he was my joy and my pleasure, he was my delight and my happiness, he was my solace and my comfort. How I ever thought on him even when I saw him not! Ah, my Love! how has this come to pass? What can have chanced to you since you have been false to me? I bethought me, God bless me! that you would be more loyal to me than was Tristram to Isoud. I loved you, may God have pity on me! far more than I did myself. Never at any time have I been guilty in thought, word, or deed, be it great or small, for the which you should hate me, or so basely betray me, as to set at naught our love to love another, and to forsake me and discover our secret. Alas, my Love! greatly do I marvel, for my heart, so help me God! was never thus toward you; for if all the world, and even all His heaven and His Paradise, had been given to me by God, I would not have taken them if for them I had had to lose you, for you were my strength and my life and my joy, and naught could have wounded me so much as that my sad heart should know that yours no longer loved me. Ah, wondrous love! Who would have thought that he could do me hurt who said, when he was with me, and I did my utmost to do all his pleasure, that he was all mine, and that he held me as his lady both in body and soul? And so sweetly did he say it unto me, that verily I believed him, nor could I in any way have thought that, for the sake of either Duchess or Queen, he could find in his heart anger and hatred against me; for such delight was it to love him, that I took his heart to mine own, and moreover I thought of him that he would be my friend all his life long, for well I knew in my heart that if he had died before me, so much did I love him, little while after him could I have dured. Better were it for me to be dead with him, than to live, if I could never see him more. Ah, wondrous love! Is it right, then, that he has made known our secret, by the which he loses me? When I freely gave him my love, I said to him, and truly made covenant with him, that whensoever he made known our love, he would lose me. And as now I have lost him, I cannot live after such sorrow, nor without him for whom I mourn, do I desire so to do. No longer have I any pleasure of my life, and so I pray God to send me death, and that as, in very truth, I have loyally loved him who has so repaid me, He may have pity on my soul, and grant that honour may come to him who has wrongfully betrayed me and delivered me over unto death, and I pardon him. And my death, meseemeth, is sweet since it comes from him, and when I have in remembrance his love, it grieves me not to die for him."

Then the Chatelaine ceased speaking, save to say with a sigh, "Sweet friend, I commend you to God." And at these words she clasped her arms tightly together, and her heart failed her, and her face changed colour, and she swooned with anguish, and lay dead in the middle of the bed, pale and without colour.

But her Love, who amused himself in the hall at the carole and the dance, knew naught of this, but naught that he saw there gave him pleasure since he saw not her to whom he had given his heart, at the which he marvelled greatly. And he whispered to the Duke: "Sire, how comes it that your niece so long while remains away, and comes not to the carole? I know not whether you have sent her to prison!"

And the Duke, who had not noticed this, cast a glance at the carole, and then he took the Knight by the hand, and straightway repaired to the chamber. And when he found her not there, he commanded and counselled

THE CHATELAINE OF VERGI

the Knight to seek her in the inner chamber, for he willed it in suchwise so that they might have solace one of another with embraces and kisses. And the Knight, who was very grateful to him for this, entered the inner chamber where his Love lay on her back on the bed, livid and without colour. And having opportunity for this, and pleasure in it, he forthwith clasped her in his arms, and kissed her, but he found that her mouth was cold, and that she was all pale and stiff, and from her appearance he saw well that she was quite dead. And at once, all aghast, he cried out: "What is it, alas? Is my Love dead?"

And the handmaiden who lay at the foot of the bed hasted to him and said: "Sire, verily do I believe that she is dead, for since she came here, she has done naught but torment herself because of the anger of her Love, and a little dog, about the which my lady had harassed and taunted her, the trouble of which has killed her."

And when the Knight heard that the words which he had spoken to the Duke had killed her, without measure was he discomforted. "Alas, my sweet Love!" said he, "the most courteous and the best and the most loyal that ever was, as a disloyal traitor I have caused your death. It would be just that on me should have fallen this fate, and that no ill should have come to you. But you had so loyal a heart, that you have taken it beforehand upon yourself. But I shall do justice upon myself because of the treachery that I have committed."

And then he drew from its sheath a sword that hung upon a nail, and ran it through his heart, and he fell on the other body, and so much did he bleed, that he died.

And the handmaiden rushed forth when she

saw the lifeless bodies. Dismayed was she at what she saw. And to the Duke, whom she met, she told all that she had heard and seen, and kept back from him naught of how the affair began, and also of the little trained dog about which the Duchess had spoken.

Then was the Duke mad with rage. And straightway he entered the chamber, and drew out of the body of the Knight the sword with the which he had killed himself. Then, without making further inquiry, he at once went with great haste straight to the carole. And forthwith he went to the Duchess, and made good his promise to her, and without uttering a word, struck her on the head with the naked sword which he held, so wrathful was he. And the Duchess fell at his feet in the sight of all those of the land, and thereat the knights who were assembled there were sore distressed, after that they had had great joy. And then the

Duke, in the hearing of all who would hear it, told the whole affair before all the Court.

And none were there who did not weep, above all when they saw the two lovers who were dead, as well as the Duchess. And the Court separated in mourning and anger and sorry confusion. And on the morrow the Duke caused the lovers to be buried in one grave, and the Duchess in another place. But from this adventure he had such sorrow, that never again was he heard to laugh. And forthwith he went on a crusade beyond the sea, from whence he returned not, for there he became a Templar.

Ah, God! All this distress and trouble came to the Knight because he so mischanced as to make known that which he ought to have kept secret, and which his Love had forbidden him to speak of so long as he would possess her love.

And from this example one ought to keep secret one's love with such great judgment, that one may always have in remembrance that to discover it avails naught, and that to hide it is of profit in every way. Whosoever does this, fears not the attacks of false and inquisitive felons who pry into the loves of others.

LA CHASTELAINE DE VERGI

LA CHASTELAINE DE VERGI

UNE maniere de gent sont
   Qui d'estre loial samblant font
Et de si bien conseil celer
Qu'il se covient en aus fier ;   4
Et quant vient qu'aucuns s'i descuevre
Tant qu'il sevent l'amor et l'uevre,
Si l'espandent par le païs
Et en font lor gas et lor ris ;   8
Si avient que cil joie en pert
Qui le conseil a descouvert,
Quar tant com l'amor est plus grant
Sont plus mari li fin amant,   12
Quant li uns d'aus de l'autre croit
Qu'il ait dit ce que celer doit ;

Et sovent tel meschief en vient
Que l'amor faillir en covient 16
A grant dolor et a vergoingne,
Si comme il avint en Borgoingne
D'un chevalier preu et hardi
Et de la dame de Vergi 20
Que li chevaliers tant ama
Que la dame li otria
Par itel couvenant s'amor
Qu'il seüst qu'a l'eure et au jor 24
Que par lui seroit descouverte
Lor amor, qu'il i avroit perte
Et de l'amor et de l'otroi
Qu'ele li avoit fet de soi. 28
Et, a cele amor otroier,
Deviserent qu'en .I. vergier
Li chevaliers toz jors vendroit
Au terme qu'ele li metroit, 32
Ne ne se mouvroit d'un anglet
De si que .I. petit chienet

LA CHASTELAINE DE VERGI

Verroit par le vergier aler,
Et lors venist sanz demorer   36
En sa chambre, et si seüst bien
Qu'a cele eure n'i avroit rien
Fors la dame tant seulement.
Ainsi le firent longuement,   40
Et fu l'amor douce et celee,
Que fors aus ne le sot riens nee.
Li chevaliers fu biaus et cointes
Et par sa valor fu acointes   44
Au duc qui Borgoingne tenoit ;
Et sovent aloit et venoit
A la cort, et tant i ala
Que la duchoise l'enama   48
Et li fist tel samblant d'amors
Que, s'il n'eüst le cuer aillors,
Bien se peüst apercevoir
Par samblant que l'amast por voir.   52
Mes quel samblant qu'el en feïst,
Li chevaliers samblant n'en fist,

Que poi ne grant s'aperceüst
Qu'ele vers li amor eüst,
Et tant qu'ele en ot grant anui,
Qu'ele parla .I. jor a lui
Et mist a reson par moz teus :
"Sire, vous estes biaus et preus,
Ce dient tuit, la Dieu merci :
Si avrïez bien deservi
D'avoir amie en si haut leu
Qu'en eüssiez honor et preu.
Que bien vous serroit tele amie !
—Ma dame," fet il, "je n'ai mie
Encore a ce mise m'entente.
—Par foi," dist ele, "longue atente
Vous porroit nuire, ce m'est vis :
Si lo que vous soiez amis
En .I. haut leu, se vous veez
Que vous i soiez bien amez."
Cil respont : " Ma dame, par foi,
Je ne sai mie bien por qoi

Vous le dites ne que ce monte,
Ne je ne sui ne duc ne conte 76
Que si hautement amer doie ;
Ne je ne sui mie a .II. doie
D'amer dame si souveraine,
Se je bien i metoie paine. 80
—Si estes," fet el, "se devient :
Mainte plus grant merveille avient
Et autele avendra encore.
Dites moi se vous savez ore 84
Se je vous ai m'amor donee,
Qui sui haute dame honoree.
Et cil respont isnel le pas :
"Ma dame, je ne le sai pas ; 88
Mes je voudroie vostre amor
Avoir par bien et par honor.
Mes de cele amor Dieus me gart
Qu'a moi n'a vous tort cele part 92
Ou la honte mon seignor gise ;
Qu'a nul fuer ne a nule guise

N'enprendroie tel mesprison
Com de fere tel desreson   96
Si vilaine et si desloial
Vers mon droit seignor natural.
—Fi ! " fet cele qui fu marie,
" Dans musars, et qui vous en prie ?   100
—Ha ! ma dame, por Dieu merci,
Bien le sai, mes tant vous en di."

Cele ne tint a lui plus plait,
Mes grant corouz et grant deshait   104
En ot au cuer, et si penssa,
S'ele puet, bien s'en vengera :
Si fu ele forment irie.
La nuit, quant ele fu couchie   108
Jouste le duc, a souspirer
Commença et puis a plorer,
Et li dus errant li demande
Que c'est qu'ele a, et li commande   112

Qu'ele li die maintenant :
"Certes," fait ele, "j'ai duel grant
De ce que ne set nus hauz hom
Qui foi li porte ne qui non, 116
Mes plus de bien et d'onor font
A ceus qui lor trahitor sont,
Et si ne s'en aperçoit nus.
—Par foi, dame, "fet soi li dus, 120
"Je ne sai por qoi vous le dites ;
Mes de tel chose sui je quites,
Qu'a nul fuer je ne norriroie
Trahitor, se je le savoie. 124
—Haez donc," fait ele, "celui,"
S'el nomma, "qui ne fina hui
De moi proier au lonc du jor
Que je li donaisse m'amor, 128
Et me dist que mout a lonc tens
Qu'il a este en cest porpens ;
Onques mes ne le m'osa dire.
Et je me porpenssai, biaus sire, 132

Tantost que je le vous diroie.
Et si puet estre chose vraie
Qu'il ait pieça a ce pensse :
De ce qu'il a aillors ame   136
Novele oïe n'en avon.
Si vous requier en guerredon
Que vostre honor si i gardoiz
Com vous savez que ce est droiz."   140
Li dus, a cui samble mout grief,
Li dist : " J'en vendrai bien a chief,
Et mout par tens, si com je cuit."

A malaise fu cele nuit   144
Li dus ; n'onques dormir ne pot
Por le chevalier qu'il amot,
Qu'il croit que cil eüst mesfait
Par droit que s'amor perdue ait ;   148
Et por ce toute nuit veilla.
L'endemain par matin leva,

Et fist celui a soi venir
Que sa fame li fet hair,   152
Sanz ce que de riens ait mespris.
Maintenant l'a a reson mis
Seul a seul, ne furent qu'eus deus :
"Certes," fait il, " ce est granz deus   156
Quant proesce avez et beaute,
Et il n'a en vous leaute !
Si m'en avez mout deceü,
Que j'ai mout longuement creü   160
Que vous fussiez de bone foi
Loiaus a tout le mains vers moi,
Que j'ai vers vous amor eüe.
Si ne sai dont vous est venue   164
Tel penssee et si trahitresse
Que proie avez la duchesse
Et requise de druerie !
Si avez fet grant tricherie,   168
Que plus vilaine n'estuet querre.
Issiez errant hors de ma terre !

Quar je vous en congie sanz doute,
Et la vous ve et desfent toute : 172
Si n'i entrez ne tant ne quant,
Que, se je des or en avant
Vous i pooie fere prendre,
Sachiez je vous feroie pendre." 176
Quant li chevaliers ce entent,
D'ire et de mautalent esprent
Si que tuit li tramblent si membre,
Que de s'amie li remembre 180
Dont il set qu'l ne puet joïr
Se n'est par aler et venir
Et par reperier ou pais
Dont li dus veut qu'il soit eschis ; 184
Et d'autre part li fet mout mal
Ce qu'a trahitor desloial
Le tient ses sires et a tort.
Si est en si grant desconfort 188
Qu'a mort se tient et a trahi :
"Sire," fet il, "por Dieu merci,

Ne creez ja ne ne penssez
Que je fusse onques si osez :   192
Ce que me metez a tort seure
Je ne penssai ne jor ne eure ;
S'a mal fet qui le vous a dit.
—Ne vous vaut riens li escondit,"   196
Fet li dus, " ne point n'en i a :
Cele meïsme conte m'a
En quel maniere et en quel guise
Vous l'avez proie et requise,   200
Comme trahitres envious ;
Et tel chose deïstes vous,
Puet estre, dont ele se test.
—Ma dame a dit ce que li plest,"   204
Fet cel qui mout estoit marriz,
" Ne m'i vaut riens li escondiz ;
Riens ne m'i vaut que j'en deïsse :
Si n'est riens que je n'en feïsse   208
Par si que j'en fusse creü,
Quar de ce n'i a riens eü.

—Si a," ce dist li dus, "par m'ame,"
A cui il souvient de sa fame, 212
Car bien cuidoit por voir savoir
Que sa fame li deïst voir,
C'onques n'oï que nus parlast
Que cil en autre lieu amast. 216
Dont dist li dus au chevalier :
"Se vous me volez afier
Par vostre leal serement
Que vous me direz vraiement 220
Ce que je vous demanderoie,
Par vostre dit certains seroie
Se vous avriiez fet ou non
Ce dont j'ai vers vous soupeçon." 224
Cil qui tout covoite et desire
A geter son seignor de l'ire
Qu'il a envers li sanz deserte,
Et qui redoute tele perte 228
Comme de guerpir la contree
Ou cele est qui plus li agree,

Respont qu'il tout sanz contredit
Fera ce que li dus a dit, 232
Qu'il ne pensse ne ne regarde
De ce dont li dus se prent garde,
Ne torment ne le lest pensser
Ce que li dus veut demander, 236
De riens fors de cele proiere :
Le serement en tel maniere
L'en fist, li dus la foi en prist ;
Et li dus maintenant li dist : 240
"Sachiez par fine verite
Que ce que je vous ai ame
Ça en arriere de fin cuer
Ne me lesse croire a nul fuer 244
De vous tel mesfet ne tel honte
Comme la duchoise me conte,
Ne tant ne le tenisse a voire,
Se ce ne le me feïst croire 248
Et me meist en grant doutance
Que j'esgart vostre contenance

Et de cointise et d'autre rien,
A qoi l'en puet savoir mout bien   252
Que vous amez ou que ce soit ;
Et quant d'aillors ne s'aperçoit
Nus qu'amez damoisele ou dame,
Je me pens que ce soit ma fame,   256
Qui me dist que vous la proiez.
Si ne puis estre desvoiez
Por rien que nus m'en puisse fere,
Que je croi qu'ainsi soit l'afere,   260
Se vous ne me dites qu'aillors
Amez en tel leu par amors
Que m'en lessiez sanz nule doute
Savoir en la verite toute.   264
Et se ce fere ne volez,
Comme parjurs vous en alez
Hors de ma terre sanz deloi ! "
Cil ne set nul conseil de soi,   268
Que le geu a parti si fort
Que l'un et l'autre tient a mort ;

Quar, s'il dit la verite pure,
Qu'il dira s'il ne se parjure, 272
A mort se tient ; s'il mesfet tant
Qu'il trespasse le couvenant
Qu'a sa dame et a s'amie a,
Il est seürs qu'il la perdra, 276
S'ele s'en puet apercevoir ;
Et s'il ne dit au duc le voir,
Parjures est et foimentie,
Et pert le païs et s'amie. 280
Mes du païs ne li chausist,
Se s'amie li remainsist
Que sor toute riens perdre crient.
Et por ce qu'ades li sovient 284
De la grant joie et du solaz
Qu'il a eü entre ses braz,
Si se pensse, s'il la messert
Et s'il par son mesfet la pert, 288
Quant o soi ne l'en puet mener,
Comment porra sanz li durer.

Si est en tel point autressi
Com li chastelains de Couci, 292
Qui au cuer n'avoit s'amor non,
Et dist en .I. vers de chançon :
Par Dieu, Amors, fort m'est a consirrer
Du dous solaz et de la compaingnie 296
Et des samblanz que m'i soloit moustrer
Cele qui m'ert et compaingne et amie :
Et quant regart sa simple cortoisie
Et les douz mos qu'a moi soloit parler, 300
Comme me puet li cuers ou cors durer ?
Quant il n'en part, certes trop est mauves.
Li chevaliers en tel angoisse
Ne set se le voir li connoisse, 304
Ou il mente et lest le païs.
Et quant il est ainsi penssis
Qu'il ne set li quels li vaut mieus,
L'eve du cuer li vient aus ieus 308
Por l'angoisse qu'il se porchace,
Et li descent aval la face,

Si qu'il en a le vis moillie.
Li dus n'en a pas le cuer lie, 312
Qui pensse qu'il i a tel chose
Que reconnoistre ne li ose.
Lors dist li dus isnel le pas :
« Bien voi que ne vous fiez pas 316
En moi tant com vous devriiez.
Cuidiez vous, se vous me disiez
Votre conseil celeement,
Que jel deïsse a nule gent ? 320
Je me leroie avant sanz faute
Trere les denz l'un avant l'autre.
—Ha ! » fet cil, « por Dieu merci, sire,
Je ne sai que je doie dire 324
Ne que je puisse devenir,
Mes je voudroie mieus morir
Que perdre ce que je perdroie,
Se le voir dit vous en avoie, 328
Et il estoit de li seü
Que l'eüsse reconneü

A jor qui fust a mon vivant ! "
Lors dist li dus : " Je vous creant   332
Seur le cors et l'ame de moi
Et sor l'amor et sor la foi
Que je vous doi sor vostre homage,
Que ja en trestout mon eage   336
N'en ert a creature nee
Par moi novele racontee
Ne samblant fet grant ne petit."
Et cil en plorant li a dit :   340
"Sire, jel vous dirai ainsi :
J'aim vostre niece de Vergi,
Et ele moi, tant c'on puet plus.
— Or me dites donc," fet li dus,   344
" Quant vous volez c'on vous en croie
Set nus fors vous dui ceste joie ? "
Et li chevaliers li respont :
"Nenil, creature del mont."   348
Et dist li dus : "Ce n'avint onques :
Comment i avenez vous donques,

Ne comment savez lieu ne tens ?
— Par foi, sire," fet cil, "par sens 352
Que je vous dirai, sanz riens tere,
Quant tant savez de nostre afere."
Lors li a toutes acontees
Ses venues et ses alees, 356
Et la couvenance premiere,
Et du petit chien la maniere.
Lors dist li dus : "Je vous requier
Que a vostre terme premier 360
Vueilliez que vostre compains soie
D'aler o vous en ceste voie,
Quar je vueil savoir sanz aloigne
Se ainsi va vostre besoingne : 364
Si n'en savra ma niece rien.
— Sire," fet il, "je l'otroi bien,
Mes qu'il ne vous griet ne anuit ;
Et sachiez bien g'irai anuit." 368
Et li dus dist qu'il i ira,
Que ja ne li anuiera,

Ainz li sera solaz et geu.
Entr'aus ont devise le leu 372
Ou assembleront tout a pie.
Si tost comme fu anuitie,
Car asses pres d'iluec estoit
Ou la niece le duc manoit. 376
Cele part tienent lor chemin
Tant qu'il sont venu au jardin,
Ou li dus ne fu pas grant piece,
Quant il vit le chienet sa niece 380
Qui s'en vint au bout du vergier
Ou il trova le chevalier,
Qui grant joie a fet au chienet.
Tantost a la voie se met 384
Li chevaliers, et le duc lait ;
Et li dus apres lui s'en vait
Pres de la chambre et ne se muet.
Iluec s'esconsse au mieus qu'il puet : 388
D'un arbre mout grant et mout large
S'estoit couvers com d'une targe

Et mout entent a lui celer.
D'iluec vit en la chambre entrer 392
Le chienet, et ainssy issir
Sa niece et contre lui venir
Hors de la chambre en .I. prael,
Et vit et oï tel apel 396
Comme ele li fist par solaz
De salut de bouche et de braz :
Et de ses biaus braz l'acola
Et plus de .C. foiz le besa 400
Ainz que feïst longue parole.
Et cil la rebese et acole,
Et li dist : "Ma dame, m'amie,
M'amor, mon cuer, ma druerie, 404
M'esperance et tout quanques j'aim,
Sachiez que j'ai eü grant faim
D'estre o vous si comme ore i sui
Trestoz jors puis que je n'i fui." 408
Ele redist : "Mon douz seignor,
Mes douz amis, ma douce amor,

Onques puis ne fu jor ne eure
Que ne m'anuiast la demeure ;
Mes ore de riens ne me dueil,
Car j'ai o moi ce que je vueil,
Quant si estes sains et haitiez.
Et li tres bien venuz soiez ! "
Et cil dist : " Et vous bien trovee ! "
Tout oï li dus a l'entree,
Qui mout pres d'aus apoiez fu ;
Sa niece a la voiz bien connu,
Si bien, et a la contenance,
Qu'or en est il fors de doutance,
Et si tient de ce la duchesse
Que dit li ot a menterresse,
Et mout li plest.   Or voit il bien
Que cil ne li a mesfet rien
De ce dont il l'a mescreü.
Ilueques s'est issi tenu
Toute la nuit, endementiers
Que la dame et li chevaliers

Dedenz la chambre en .I. lit furent
Et sans dormir ensemble jurent   432
A tel joie et a tel deport
Qu'il n'est resons que nus recort
Ne ne le die ne ne l'oie,
S'il n'atent a avoir tel joie   436
Comme amors a fin amant done,
Quant sa peine reguerredone ;
Quar cil qui tel joie n'atent,
S'il l'ooit or, riens n'i entent   440
Puis qu'il n'a a amors le cuer,
Que nus ne savroit a nul fuer
Combien vaut a tel joie avoir,
S'amors ne li fesoit savoir ;   444
Ne teus biens n'avient mie a touz,
Que ce est joie sanz corouz
Et solaz et envoiseüre ;
Mes tant i a que petit dure,   448
C'est avis a l'amant qui l'a,
Ja tant longues ne durera ;

Tant li plest la vie qu'il maine,
Que se nuit devenoit semaine 45
Et semaine devenoit mois,
Et mois uns anz et uns anz trois,
Et troi an .xx. et vint an cent,
Quant vendroit au definement, 45
Si voudroit il qu'il anuitast
Cele nuit, ainz qu'il ajornast.
Et en itel pensse estoit
Icil que li dus atendoit ; 46(
Quar ainz jor aler l'en covint,
Et s'amie o lui a l'uis vint.
La vit li dus au congie prendre
Besier doner et besier rendre, 46,
Et oï forment souspirer
Et au congie prendre plorer.
Iluec ot plore mainte lerme,
Et si oï prendre le terme 46!
Du rassambler iluec arriere.
Li chevaliers en tel maniere

S'en part, et la dame l'uis clot ;
Mes tant comme veoir le pot, 472
Le convoia a ses biaus ieus,
Quant ele ne pot fere mieus.

Quant li dus vit clorre l'uisset,
Tantost a la voie se met 476
Tant que le chevalier ataint
Qui a soi meïsme se plaint
De la nuit : si comme il a dit,
Trop li avoit dure petit. 480
Et tel penssee et auteus diz
Ot cele dont il ert partiz,
A cui il samble por la nuit
Que failli ait a son deduit, 484
Ne du jor ne se loe point.
Li chevaliers ert en tel point
Et de penssee et de parole,
Quant li dus l'ataint ; si l'acole 488

88 LA CHASTELAINE DE VERGI

Et li a fet joie mout grant,
Pius li a dit : " Je vous creant
Que toz jors mes vous amerai
Ne james jor ne vous harrai, 49
Quar vous m'avez du tout voir dit
Et ne m'avez de mot mentit.
—Sire, " fet cil," vostre merci !
Mes por Dieu vous requier et pri 49
Que cest conseil celer vous plaise,
Qu' amor perdroie et joie et aise
Et morroie sanz nule faute,
Se je savoie que nul autre 50
Ice savroit fors vous sanz plus.
—Or n'en parlez ja," fet li dus ;
" Sachiez qu'il ert si bien cele
Que ja par moi n'en ert parle." 50.

Ainsi s'en sont parlant venu
La dont il estoient meü.

Et cel jor quant vint au mengier,
Moustra li dus au chevalier 508
Plus biau samblant qu'ainz n'avoit fait,
Dont tel corouz et tel deshait
En ot la duchoise sanz fable
Qu'ele se leva de la table 512
Et a fet samblant par faintise
Que maladie li soit prise :
Alee est couchier en son lit
Ou ele ot petit de delit. 516
Et li dus, quant il ot mengie
Et lave et bien festoie,
Si l'est tantost alez veoir
Et la fist sus son lis seoir, 520
Et a commandé que nului
Ne remaingne leenz fors lui.
L'en fet tantost ce qu'il commande.
Et li dus errant li demande 524
Comment cist maus li est venu
Et que ce est qu'ele a eü.

Ele respont : "Se Dieus me gart,
Je ne m'en donoie regart 528
Orains, quant au mengier m'assis,
Que greignor sens et plus d'avis
N'eüst en vous que je n'i vi,
Quant vous tenez plus chier celui 532
Que je vous ai dit qui porchace
Qu'il a moi honte et despit face ;
Et quant vi que plus biau samblant
Li feïstes que de devant, 536
Si grant duel et si grant ire oi
Qu'ilueques demourer ne poi.
—Ha," fet li dus, "ma douce amie,
Sachiez je n'en croiroie mie 540
Ne vous ne autre creature
Que onques por nule aventure
Avenist ce que vous me dites ;
Ainz sai bien qu'il en est toz quites, 544
N'onques ne penssa de ce fere,
Tant ai apris de son afere :

Si ne m'en enquerez ja plus."

Atant se part d'iluec li dus ; 548
Et ele remest mout penssive
Que james tant com ele vive
Une eure a aise ne sera
Devant que plus apris avra 552
De ce dont li dus li desfent
Qu'ele ne li demant noient,
Mais ja ne l'en tendra desfensse,
Quar en son cuer engin porpensse 556
Qu'ele le porra bien savoir,
S'ele se sueffre jusqu'au soir,
Qu'ele ait le duc entre ses braz :
Ele set bien qu'en tel solaz 560
En fera, lors n'en doute point,
Mieus son vouloir qu'en autre point.
Por ce adonc a tant se tint,
Et quant li dus couchier se vint, 564

A une part du lit s'est traite;
Samblant fet que point ne li haite
Que li dus o li gesir doie,
Qu'ele set bien ce est la voie   568
De son mari metre au desouz
Par fere semblant de corouz.
Por ce se tint en itel guise
Afin que mieus le duc atise   572
A croire que mout soit irie;
Por ce sanz plus qu'il l'a besie
Li dist ele: "Mout estes faus
Et trichierres et desloiaus,   576
Qui moi moustrez samblant d'amor,
N'onques ne m'amastes nul jor;
Et j'ai este lonc tens si fole
Que j'ai creü vostre parole   580
Que soventes foiz disiez,
Que de cuer loial m'amiiez;
Mes hui m'en sui aperceüe
Que j'en ai este deceüe."   584

Et li dus dist : "Et vous a qoi ?
—Ja me deïstes par ma foi,"
Fet cele qui a mal i bee,
"Que je ne fusse si osee 588
Que je vous enquerisse rien
De ce que or savez vous bien.
—De qoi, suer, savez vous, por De ?
—De ce que cil vous a conte," 592
Fet ele, "mençonge et arvoire,
Qu'il vous a fet pensser et croire.
Mes de ce savoir ne me chaut,
Que j'ai pensse que petit vaut 596
A vous amer de cuer loial,
Que c'onques fust ou bien ou mal,
Mes cuers riens ne vit ne ne sot
Que ne seüssiez ausi tost ; 600
Et or voi que vous me celez,
Vostre merci, les voz penssez.
Si sachiez ore sanz doutance
Que james n'avrai tel fiance 604

En vous ne cuer de tel maniere
Com j'ai eü ça en arriere."
Lors a commencié a plorer
La duchoise et a souspirer, 608
Et s'esforça plus qu'ele pot.
Et li dus tel pitie en ot
Qu'il li a dit : " Ma bele suer,
Je ne soufferroie a nul fuer 612
Ne vostre corouz ne vostre ire ;
Mes sachiez je ne puis pas dire
Ce que volez que je vous die
Sanz fere trop grant vilonie." 616
Ele respont isnel le pas :
" Sire, si ne m'en dites pas,
Quar je voi bien a cel samblant
Qu'en moi ne vous fiez pas tant 620
Que celaisse vostre conseil ;
Et sachiez que mout me merveil :
Ainc n'oïstes grant ne petit
Conseil que vous m'eüssiez dit, 624

Dont descouvers fussiez par moi,
Et si vous di en bone foi,
Ja en ma vie n'avendra."
Quant ce ot dit, si replora ; 628
Et li dus si l'acole et bese,
Et est de son cuer a malese
Si que plus ne se pot tenir
De sa volente descouvrir. 632
Puis si li a dit : "Bele dame,
Je ne sai que face per m'ame,
Que tant m'afi en vous et croi
Que chose celer ne vous doi 636
Que je sache, mes trop me dot
Que vous n'en parlez aucun mot :
Sachiez, et itant vous en di,
Que se je sui par vous trahi, 640
Vous en receverez la mort."
Et ele dist : " Bien m'i acort ;
Estre ne porroit que feïsse
Chose dont vers vous mespreïsse." 644

Cil qui l'aime por ce le croit
Et cuide que veritez soit
De ce que li dist, puis li conte
De sa niece trestout le conte, 648
Comme apris l'ot du chevalier,
Et comment il fu el vergier
En l'anglet ou il n'ot qu'eus deus,
Quant li chienes s'en vint a eus; 652
Et de l'issue et de l'entree
Li a la verite contee,
Si qu'il ne li a riens teü
Qu'il i ait oï ne veü. 656
Et quant la duchoise l'entent
Que cil aime plus bassement
Qui de s'amor l'a escondite,
Morte se tient et a despite, 660
Mes ainc de ce samblant ne fist,
Ainçois otroia et promist
Au duc a si celer ceste uevre ;
Se ce est qu'ele le descuevre, 664

Que l'en la pende a une hart.

Et si li est il ja mout tart
D'a celi parler qu'ele het
Des icele heure qu'ele set 668
Que ele est amie a celui
Qui li fet et honte et anui
Por itant, ce li est avis,
Qu'il ne vout estre ses amis. 672
Si afferme tout son porpens
Que, s'ele voit ne lieu ne tens
· Qu'a la niece le duc parolt,
Qu'ele li dira ausi tost, 676
Ne ja ne celera tel chose
Ou felonie avra enclose.
Mes ainc en point n'en lieu n'en vint
Tant qu'a la Pentecouste vint 680
Que ce fu la feste premiere,
Que li dus tint cort mout pleniere,

Si qu'il envoia par tout querre
Toutes les dames de la terre 684
Et sa niece tout premeraine
Qui de Vergi ert chastelaine.
Et quant la duchoise la vit,
Tantost toz li sans li fremist, 688
Com cele del mont que plus het.
Mes son corage celer set :
Si li a fet plus bel atret
C'onques devant ne li ot fet ; 692
Mes mout ot grant talent de dire
Ce dont ele ot au cuer grant ire,
Et la demeure mout li couste.
Por ce, le jour de Pentecouste, 696
Quant les tables furent ostees,
En a la duchoise menees
Les dames en sa chambre o soi
Por eles parer en reqoi, 700
Por venir cointes aus caroles.
Lors ne pot garder ses paroles

La duchoise qui vit son leu,
Ainz dist ausi comme par geu : 704
"Chastelaine, soiez bien cointe,
Quar bel et preu avez acointe."
Et cele respont simplement :
"Je ne sai quel acointement 708
Vous penssez, ma dame, por voir,
Que talent n'ai d'ami avoir
Qui ne soit del tout a l'onor
Et de moi et de mon seignor. 712
.— Je l'otroi bien," dit la duchesse,
"Mais vous estes bone mestresse,
Qui avez apris le mestier
Du petit chienet afetier." 716

Les dames ont oï le conte,
Mes ne sevent a qoi ce monte ;
O la duchoise s'en revont
Aus caroles qui fetes sont. 720

Et la chastelaine remaint:
Li cuers li trouble d'ire et taint
Et li mue trestoz el ventre.
Dedenz une garderobe entre   724
Ou une pucelete estoit
Qui aus piez du lit se gisoit,
Mes ele ne la pot veoir.
Dedenz le lit se lest cheoir   728
La chastelaine mout dolente;
Iluec se plaint et se gaimente,
Et dist: "Ha! sire Dieus, merci,
Que puet estre que j'ai oï   732
Que ma dame m'a fet regret
Que j'ai afetie mon chienet?
Ce ne set ele par nului,
Ce sai je bien, fors par celui   736
Que j'amoie et trahie m'a;
Ne ce ne li deïst il ja,
S'a li n'eüst grant acointance,
Et s'il ne l'amast sanz doutance 740

Plus que moi quant il m'a trahie !
Mais or voi qu'il ne m'aime mie,
Quant il me faut de couvenant.
Douz Dieus ! et je l'amoie tant   744
Comme riens peüst autre amer,
Qu'aillors ne pooie pensser
Nis une eure ne jor ne nuit !
Quar c'ert ma joie et mon deduit,   748
C'ert mes delis, c'ert mes depors,
C'ert mes solaz, c'ert mes confors.
Comment a lui me contenoie
De pensser, quant je nel veoie !   752
Ha ! amis, dont est ce venu ?
Que poez estre devenu,
Quant vers moi avez esté faus ?
Je cuidoie que plus loiaus   756
Me fussiez, se Dieus me conseut,
Que ne fust Tristans a Yseut ;
Plus vous amoie la moitié,
Se Dieus ait ja de moi pitié,   760

Que ne fesoie moi meïsmes ;
Onques avant, ne puis ne primes
En pensser n'en dit ne en fet
Ne fis ne poi ne grant mesfet   764
Par qoi me deüssiez haïr
Ne si vilainement trahir
Comme a noz amors depecier
Por autre amer et moi lessier,   768
Et descouvrir nostre conseil.
He ! lasse, amis, mout me merveil,
Que li miens cuers, si m'aït Dieus,
Ne fu onques vers vous itieus.   772
Car, se tout le mont et neïs
Tout son ciel et son paradis
Me donast Dieus, pas nes preïsse
Par couvenant que vous perdisse ;   776
Quar vous estiiez ma richece
Et ma santez et ma leece,
Ne riens grever ne me peüst
Tant comme mes las cuers seüst   780

Que li vostres de riens m'amast.
Ha! fine amor! et qui penssast
Que cist feist vers moi desroi,
Qui disoit, quant il ert o moi 784
Et je fesoie mon pooir
De fere trestout son voloir,
Qu'il ert toz miens, et a sa dame
Me tenoit et de cors et d'ame, 788
Et le disoit si doucement
Que le creoie vraiement,
Ne je ne penssaisse a nul fuer
Qu'il peüst trover en son cuer 792
Envers moi corouz ne haine
Por duchoise ne por roine ;
Qu'a lui amer estoit si buen
Qu'a mon cuer prenoie le suen ; 796
De lui me penssoie autressi
Qu'il se tenoit a mon ami
Toute sa vie et son eage,
Quar bien connois a mon corage, 800

S'avant morust, que tant l'amaisse
Que petit apres lui duraisse.
Estre morte o lui me fust mieus
Que vivre si que de mes ieus 804
Ne le veïsse nule foiz.
Ha! fine amor, est ce donc droiz
Que cil a ainsi descouvert
Nostre conseil, dont il me pert? 808
Qu'a m'amor otroier li dis
Et bien en couvenant li mis
Qu' a icele eure me perdroit
Que nostre amor descovreroit. 812
Et quant j'ai avant perdu lui,
Ne puis vivre apres tel anui.
Que sanz lui por cui je me dueil
Ne puis vivre ne je ne vueil; 816
De ma vie ne me plest point,
Ainz pri Dieu que la mort me doinst,
Et que, tout ausi vraiement
Comme j'ai ame leaument 820

Celui qui ce m'a porchacié,
Ait de l'ame de moi pitié,
Et a celui qui a son tort
M'a trahie et livrée a mort   824
Doinst honor. Et je li pardon ;
Ne ma mort n'est se douce non,
Ce m'est avis, quant de lui vient ;
Et quant de s'amor me sovient,   828
Por lui morir ne m'est pas paine."

A tant se tut la chastelaine
Fors qu'ele dist en souspirant :
"Douz amis, a Dieu vous commant !"   832
A cest mot de ses braz s'estraint,
Li cuers li faut, li vis li taint :
Angoisseusement s'est pasmee,
Et gist pale et descoloree   836
En mi le lit, morte, sanz vie.
Mes ses amis ne le set mie,

Qui se deduisoit en la sale
A la carole et dansse et bale ; 840
Mes ne li plest riens qu'il i voie,
Quant cele a cui son cuer s'otroie
N'i voit point, dont mout se merveille.
Si a dit au duc en l'oreille : 844
"Sire, qu'est ce que vostre niece
Est demoree si grant piece,
Que n'est aus caroles venue ?
Ne sai se l'avez mise en mue." 848
Et li dus la carole esgarde,
Qui de ce ne s'estoit pris garde :
Celui a soi par la main trait,
Et droit en la chambre s'en vait ; 852
Et quant illueques ne la trueve,
Au chevalier commande et rueve
Qu'en la garderobe la quiere,
Quar il le veut en tel maniere, 856
Por leenz entr'aus solacier
Com d'acoler et de besier.

Et cil qui li en sot hauz grez
Est en la garderobe entrez 860
Ou s'amie gisoit enverse
El lit, descolouree et perse.
Cil maintenant l'acole et baise,
Que bien en ot et lieu et aise ; 864
Mes la bouche a trovee froide
Et partout bien pale et bien roide,
Et au samblant que li cors moustre
Voit bien qu'ele est morte tout outre. 868
Tantost toz esbahiz s'escrie :
"Qu'est ce, las ? est morte m'amie ?"
Et la pucele sailli sus
Qui aus piez du lit gisoit jus, 872
Et dist : "Sire, ce croi je bien
Qu'ele soit morte, qu'autre rien
Ne demanda puis que vint ci,
Por le corouz de son ami 876
Dont ma dame l'ataïna
Et d'un chienet la ramposna,

Dont li corouz li vint morteus."
Et quant cil entent les mos teus   880
Que ce qu'il dist au duc l'a morte,
Sanz mesure se desconforte :
"Ha las !" dist il, "ma douce amor,
La plus cortoise et la meillor   884
C'onques fust et la plus loial,
Comme trichierres desloial
Vous ai morte !   Si fust droiture
Que sor moi tornast l'aventure,   888
Si que vous n'en eüssiez mal ;
Mes le cuer aviez si loial
Que sor vous l'avez avant prise.
Mes je ferai de moi justise   892
Por la trahison que j'ai fete !"
Une espee du fuerre a trete
Qui ert pendue a .I. espuer,
Et s'en feri par mi le cuer :   896
Cheoir se lest sor l'autre cors ;
Cil a tant sainie qu'il est mors.

Et la pucele est hors saillie,
Quant ele vit les cors sanz vie : 900
Hidor ot de ce qu'ele vit.
Au duc qu'ele encontra a dit
Ce qu'ele a oï et veü
Si qu'ele n'i a riens teü, 904
Comment l'afere ert commencie,
Neïs du chienet afetie
Dont la Duchoise avoit parle.
Ez vous le duc adonc derve : 908
Tout maintenant en la chambre entre,
Au chevalier trest fors du ventre
L'espee dont s'estoit ocis.
Tantost s'est a la voie mis 912
Grant oirre droit a la carole,
Sanz plus tenir longue parole ;
Maintenant vint a la duchesse :
Si li a rendu sa promesse 916
Quar el chief li a embatue
L'espee qu'il aportoit nue,

Sanz parler, tant estoit iriez.
La duchoise chiet a ses piez, 920
Voiant toz ceus de la contree,
Dont fu la feste mout troublee
Des chevaliers qui la estoient,
Qui grant joie menee avoient. 924
Et li dus trestout ausi tost,
Oiant toz, qui oïr le vost,
Conta l'afere en mi la cort.
Lors n'i a celui qui n'en plort, 928
Et nommeement quant il voient
Les .II. amanz qui mort estoient,
Et la duchoise d'autre part :
A duel et a corouz depart 932
La cort et a meschief vilain.
Li dus enterrer l'endemain
Fist les amanz en .I. sarqueu,
Et la duchoise en autre leu. 936
Mes de l'aventure ot tele ire
C'onques puis ne l'oï on rire.

Errant se croisa d'outre mer,
Ou il ala sanz retorner, 940
Si devint ilueques Templiers.
Ha! Dieus! trestous cilz encombriers
Et cis meschies por ce avint
Qu'au chevalier tant mesavint 944
Qu'il dist ce que celer devoit
Et que desfendu li avoit
S'amie qu'il ne le deïst
Tant com s'amor avoir vousist. 948
Et par cest example doit l'en
S'amor celer par si grant sen
C'on ait toz jors en remembrance
Que li descouvrirs riens n'avance. 952
Et li celers en toz poins vaut.
Qui si le fait, ne crient assaut
Des faus felons enquerreors,
Qui enquierent autrui amors. 956

Printed by BALLANTINE, HANSON & Co.
Edinburgh & London

A CONCISE LIST OF

THE KING'S CLASSICS

GENERAL EDITOR: PROFESSOR I. GOLLANCZ, Litt.D.

ALTHOUGH The King's Classics are to be purchased for 1/6 net per volume, the series is unique in that

(1) the letterpress, paper, and binding are unapproached by any similar series.

(2) "Competent scholars in every case have supervised this series, which can therefore be received with confidence."—*Athenæum*.

(3) With few exceptions, the volumes in this series are included in no similar series, while several are copyright.

THE KING'S CLASSICS

UNDER THE GENERAL EDITORSHIP OF PROFESSOR I. GOLLANCZ, LITT.D.

"Right Royal Series."—*Literary World.*

"We note with pleasure that competent scholars in every case have supervised this series, which can therefore be received with confidence."—*Athenæum.*

"The name of Professor I. Gollancz has been at various times associated with a large number of noteworthy works in literature, but it is doubtful whether he has ever done a finer, yet less obtrusive, work of popular education than that associated with his general editorship of 'The King's Classics.' . . . This venture has important and well-defined aims. It seeks to introduce many important works of literature that have not been readily accessible in a cheap form, or not hitherto rendered into English. It stands first and last for pure scholarship. Each volume is edited by some expert scholar, and contains a summary introduction, dealing with the principal facts of the literary history of the book; while at the end are added copious explanatory notes and a carefully-compiled index. Never is the man who reads to learn forgotten.

At the same time modern popular classics, more especially such as have not yet been adequately or at all annotated, are not excluded from the series. In fact, 'The King's Classics' are in the main representative of Professor Gollancz's own ideal of what such a library should be, for here and there it will be observed with pleasure that he steps deliberately out of the ordinary track, and includes in his series several modern but invaluable books that have never seen printer's ink under similar auspices. . . .

· The literary importance of these volumes cannot be questioned, and when it is added that each is bound in a peculiarly effective scheme of grey blue and white imitation vellum, all people who love dainty associations with the *format* of their books should remember that 'The King's Classics' have every claim for their consideration and approval."—*Standard.*

THE KING'S CLASSICS

The "King's Classics" are printed on antique laid paper, 16mo. (6 × 4½ inches), gilt tops, and are issued in the following styles and prices. Each volume has a frontispiece, usually in photogravure.

Quarter bound, antique grey boards, **1/6** net.
Red Cloth, **1/6** net.
Quarter Vellum, grey cloth sides, **2/6** net.
Special three-quarter Vellum, Oxford side-papers, gilt tops, silk marker, **5/-** net.

⁎ Nos. 2, 20 and 24 are double volumes. Price, Boards or Cloth, **3/-** net; Quarter Vellum, **5/-** net; special three-quarter Vellum, **7/6** net.

NOTE.—*In response to many applications, the publishers have arranged to supply school-masters requiring volumes in this series for class use with not fewer than 25 copies of any one title, in stout paper covers, price 1/- net. Double volumes 2/- net.*

SHORT LIST

ARRANGED ALPHABETICALLY IN ORDER OF AUTHORS' NAMES.

APULEIUS, Cupid and Psyche, etc., in ADLINGTON'S translation. No. 12.

ASSER, The Life of King Alfred. No. 57.

BENET (SAINT), The Rule of. No. 59.

BONIFACE (SAINT), English Correspondence of. No. 53.

BROWNING (ROBERT), Men and Women. 2 *vols*. Nos. 26, 27.

BURY (RICHARD DE), The Love of Books (Philobiblon). No. 1.

CALDERON, Six Dramas of. Translated by EDWARD FITZGERALD. *Double volume.* No. 2.

CAVALIER TO HIS LADY, THE. No. 56.

CHARLEMAGNE, Early Lives of. No. 22.

THE KING'S CLASSICS

CHAUCER, The Prologue, and Minor Poems. *In modern English by* Professor SKEAT. No 47.
CHAUCER, The Knight's Tale.   *In modern English.* No. 8.
CHAUCER, The Man of Law's Tale, etc.   „   „   No. 9.
CHAUCER, The Prioress's Tale, etc.   „   „   No. 10.
CHAUCER, The Legend of Good Women „   „   No. 41.
CHAUCER, The Parliament of Birds, and the House of Fame. *In modern English.* No. 48.
CICERO, Friendship, Old Age, and Scipio's Dream. No. 23.
DANIEL and DRAYTON, Delia and Idea. No. 60.
DANTE, The Vita Nuova. Italian text with D. G. ROSSETTI's translation on the opposite pages. No. 46.
DANTE, Early Lives of. No. 14.
DEKKER (THOMAS), The Gull's Hornbook. No. 19.
EIKON BASILIKE. No. 5.
ELIOT (GEORGE), Silas Marner. No. 30.
EVELYN (JOHN), The Life of Margaret Godolphin. No. 13.
FITZGERALD (EDWARD), Polonius. No. 16.   [See *Calderon.*
FULK FITZ-WARINE, The Romance of. No. 11.
GASKELL (MRS.), Cranford. No. 49.
GOLDSMITH, The Vicar of Wakefield. No. 31.
ICELANDIC, TRANSLATIONS FROM THE. No. 58.
JOCELYN OF BRAKELOND, The Chronicle of. No. 3.
KINGS' LETTERS. Nos. 6, 7, 51, 52.
LAMB (CHARLES), The Essays of Elia. *Two volumes.* Nos. 54, 55.
LANGLAND, The Vision of Piers the Plowman. *In moaern English by* Professor SKEAT. No. 18.

6   THE KING'S CLASSICS

MANNING (MISS), The Household of Sir Thomas More. No. 33.
MEDIÆVAL LORE. No. 17.
MONMOUTH, Memoirs of Robert Cary, Earl of. No. 21.
MORE (SIR THOMAS), Utopia. No. 40.
MORE (SIR THOMAS), The Four Last Things. No. 44.
MORRIS (WILLIAM), The Defence of Guenevere, etc. No. 25.
NUN's RULE, The, or Ancren Riwle. *In modern English. Double volume.* No. 20.
PEARL. With a translation into Modern English by Professor I. GOLLANCZ. No. 50.
PETTIE (GEORGE), The Petite Pallace of Pettie his Pleasure. *Two volumes.* Nos. 36, 37.
POE (E. A.), Poems. No. 28.
POETS ROYAL OF ENGLAND AND SCOTLAND. No. 39.
READE (CHARLES), Peg Woffington. No. 32.
ROLAND, THE SONG OF. No. 45.
ROPER (WILLIAM), The Life of Sir Thomas More. No. 4.
SAPPHO: One Hundred Lyrics. By BLISS CARMAN. No. 34.
SHAKESPEARE, The Sonnets. No. 29.
SWIFT, The Battle of the Books, with Extracts from the Literature of the Phalaris Controversy. No. 42.
SYMONDS (J. A.), Wine, Women, and Song. No. 35.
TEMPLE (SIR W.), On the Gardens of Epicurus, with other 17th Century Garden Essays. No. 43.
WALPOLE (HORACE), The Castle of Otranto. No. 38.
WHITE (JAMES), The Falstaff Letters. No. 15.
WORDSWORTH, The Prelude. *Double volume.* No. 24.

THE KING'S CLASSICS

DETAILED LIST

1. **THE LOVE OF BOOKS**: being the Philobiblon of RICHARD DE BURY.
   Translated by E. C. THOMAS. Frontispiece, Seal of Richard de Bury (as Bishop of Durham).

2. **SIX DRAMAS OF CALDERON.**
   Translated by EDWARD FITZGERALD. Editor, H. OELSNER, M.A., Ph.D. Frontispiece, Portrait of Calderon, from an etching by M. EGUSQUIZA. [*Double volume.*

3. **THE CHRONICLE OF JOCELIN OF BRAKELOND, MONK OF ST. EDMUNDS BURY**: a Picture of Monastic and Social Life in the XIIth Century.
   Newly translated, from the original Latin, with notes, table of dates relating to the Abbey of St. Edmundsbury, and index, by L. C. JANE, M.A. Introduction by the Right Rev. Abbot GASQUET. Frontispiece, Seal of Abbot Samson (A.D. 1200). (See No. 20.)

4. **THE LIFE OF SIR THOMAS MORE**, Knight.
   By his son-in-law, WILLIAM ROPER. With letters to and from his famous daughter, Margaret Roper. Frontispiece, Portrait of Sir Thomas More, after Holbein.

5. **EIKON BASILIKE**: or, The King's Book.
   Edited by EDWARD ALMACK, F.S.A. Frontispiece, Portrait of King Charles I. This edition, which has been printed from an advance copy of the King's Book seized by Cromwell's soldiers, is the first inexpensive one for a hundred years in which the original spelling of the first edition has been preserved.

THE KING'S CLASSICS

6, 7. KINGS' LETTERS.
Part I. Letters of the Kings of England, from Alfred to the Coming of the Tudors, newly edited from the originals by ROBERT STEELE, F.S.A. Frontispiece, Portrait of Henry V.

Part II. From the Early Tudors, with the love-letters of Henry VIII. and Anne Boleyn, and with frontispiece, Portrait of Anne Boleyn. (See also Nos. 51, 52.)

8. CHAUCER'S KNIGHT'S TALE, or Palamon and Arcite.
In modern English by Professor SKEAT, Litt.D. Frontispiece, "The Canterbury Pilgrims," from an illuminated MS.

9. CHAUCER'S MAN OF LAW'S TALE, Squire's Tale, and Nun's Priest's Tale.
In modern English by Professor SKEAT, Litt.D. Frontispiece from an illuminated MS.

10. CHAUCER'S PRIORESS'S TALE, Pardoner's Tale, Clerk's Tale, and Canon's Yeoman's Tale.
In modern English by Professor SKEAT, Litt.D. Frontispiece, "The Patient Griselda," from the well-known fifteenth-century picture of the Umbrian School in the National Gallery.

11. THE ROMANCE OF FULK FITZ-WARINE.
Newly translated from the Anglo-French by ALICE KEMP-WELCH, with an introduction by Professor BRANDIN. Frontispiece, Whittington Castle in Shropshire, the seat of the Fitzwarines.

12. THE STORY OF CUPID AND PSYCHE.
From "The Golden Ass" of Apuleius, translated by W. ADLINGTON (1566), edited by W. H. D. ROUSE, Litt.D. With frontispiece representing the "Marriage of Cupid and Psyche," after a gem now in the British Museum.

THE KING'S CLASSICS

13. **THE LIFE OF MARGARET GODOLPHIN.**
By JOHN EVELYN, the famous diarist. Re-edited from the edition of Samuel Wilberforce, Bishop of Oxford. Frontispiece, Portrait of Margaret Godolphin engraved on copper.

14. **EARLY LIVES OF DANTE.**
Comprising Boccaccio's Life of Dante, Leonardo Bruni's Life of Dante, and other important contemporary records. Translated and edited by the Rev. PHILIP H. WICKSTEED. Frontispiece, The Death-mask of Dante.

15. **THE FALSTAFF LETTERS.**
By JAMES WHITE, possibly with the assistance of CHARLES LAMB, *cf. the Introduction*. Frontispiece, Sir John Falstaff dancing to Master Brooks' fiddle, from the original edition.

16. **POLONIUS, a Collection of Wise Saws and Modern Instances.**
By EDWARD FITZGERALD. With portrait of Edward Fitz-Gerald from the miniature by Mrs. E. M. B. RIVETT-CARNAC as frontispiece; notes and index. Contains a preface by EDWARD FITZGERALD, on Aphorisms generally.

17. **MEDIÆVAL LORE.**
From Bartholomæus Anglicus. Edited with notes, index and glossary by ROBERT STEELE. Preface by the late WILLIAM MORRIS. Frontispiece, an old illumination, representing Astrologers using Astrolabes.
The book is drawn from one of the most widely-read works of mediæval times. Its popularity is explained by its scope, which comprises explanations of allusions to natural objects met with in Scripture and elsewhere. It was, in fact, an account of the properties of things in general.

18. **THE VISION OF PIERS THE PLOWMAN.**
By WILLIAM LANGLAND; *in modern English by* Professor SKEAT, Litt.D. Frontispiece, "God Speed the Plough," from an old MS.

THE KING'S CLASSICS

19. THE GULL'S HORNBOOK.
By Thomas Dekker. Editor, R. B. McKerrow. Frontispiece, The nave of St. Paul's Cathedral at the time of Elizabeth.

20. THE NUN'S RULE, or Ancren Riwle, in Modern English. [*Double volume.*
Being the injunctions of Bishop Poore intended for the guidance of nuns or anchoresses, as set forth in this famous thirteenth-century MS.
Editor, the Right Rev. Abbot Gasquet. Frontispiece, Seal of Bishop Poore. (See Nos. 3, 59.)

21. THE MEMOIRS OF ROBERT CARY, Earl of Monmouth.
Being a contemporary record of the life of that nobleman as Warden of the Marches and at the Court of Elizabeth.
Editor, G. H. Powell. With frontispiece from the original edition, representing Queen Elizabeth in a state procession, with the Earl of Monmouth and others in attendance.

22. EARLY LIVES OF CHARLEMAGNE.
Translated and edited by A. J. Grant. With frontispiece representing an early bronze figure of Charlemagne from the Musée Carnavalet, Paris.
We have here given us two "Lives" of Charlemagne by contemporary authorities—one by Eginhard and the other by the Monk of St. Gall. Very different in style, when brought together in one volume each supplies the deficiencies of the other.

23. CICERO'S "FRIENDSHIP," "OLD AGE," AND "SCIPIO'S DREAM."
From early translations. Editor, W. H. D. Rouse, Litt.D. Frontispiece, "Scipio, Laelius and Cato conversing," from a fourteenth-century MS.

THE KING'S CLASSICS

24. WORDSWORTH'S PRELUDE.
The introduction and notes have been written by W. BASIL WORSFOLD, M.A., and the frontispiece is taken from the portrait of Wordsworth by H. W. PICKERSGILL, R.A., in the National Gallery. A map of the Lake District is added.
[*Double volume.*

25. THE DEFENCE OF GUENEVERE and other Poems by WILLIAM MORRIS.
Editor, ROBERT STEELE. With reproduction of DANTE GABRIEL ROSSETTI's picture of "Lancelot and Guenevere at King Arthur's tomb" as frontispiece.

26, 27. BROWNING'S "MEN AND WOMEN."
Edited with introduction and notes by W. BASIL WORSFOLD, M.A. Two volumes, each with portrait of Browning as frontispiece.
[*In two volumes.*

28. POE'S POEMS.
Editor, EDWARD HUTTON. Frontispiece, Drawing of Poe's cottage.

29. SHAKESPEARE'S SONNETS.
Editor, Mrs. C. C. STOPES. Frontispiece, Portrait of the Earl of Southampton.

30. GEORGE ELIOT'S SILAS MARNER.
Frontispiece, Portrait of George Eliot, from a water-colour drawing by Mrs. CHARLES BRAY. Introduction by RICHARD GARNETT.

31. GOLDSMITH'S VICAR OF WAKEFIELD.
Introduction by RICHARD GARNETT. Frontispiece, Portrait of Oliver Goldsmith.

32. CHARLES READE'S PEG WOFFINGTON.
Frontispiece, Portrait of Peg Woffington. Introduction by RICHARD GARNETT.

THE KING'S CLASSICS

33. THE HOUSEHOLD OF SIR THOMAS MORE.
By ANNE MANNING. Preface by RICHARD GARNETT. Frontispiece, "The Family of Sir Thomas More."

34. SAPPHO : One Hundred Lyrics.
By BLISS CARMAN. With frontispiece after a Greek gem.

35. WINE, WOMEN, AND SONG.
Mediæval students' songs, translated from the Latin, with an essay, by JOHN ADDINGTON SYMONDS. Frontispiece after a fifteenth-century woodcut.

36, 37. GEORGE PETTIE'S "PETITE PALLACE OF PETTIE HIS PLEASURE."
The popular Elizabethan book containing twelve classical love-stories—"Sinorix and Camma," "Tereus and Progne," etc.—in style the precursor of Euphues, now first reprinted under the editorship of Professor I. GOLLANCZ. Frontispieces, a reproduction of the original title-page, and of a page of the original text. [*In two volumes.*

38. WALPOLE'S CASTLE OF OTRANTO.
The introduction of Sir WALTER SCOTT. Preface by Miss C. SPURGEON. Frontispiece, Portrait of Walpole, after a contemporary engraving.

39. THE POETS ROYAL OF ENGLAND AND SCOTLAND.
Being Original Poems by English Kings and other Royal and Noble Persons, now first collected and edited by W. BAILEY-KEMPLING. Frontispiece, Portrait of King James I. of Scotland, after an early engraving.

THE KING'S CLASSICS

40. SIR THOMAS MORE'S UTOPIA.
Now for the first time edited in modern spelling from *the first English edition*, with notes and bibliography by ROBERT STEELE. Frontispiece, Portrait of Sir Thomas More, after an early engraving.

41. CHAUCER'S LEGEND OF GOOD WOMEN.
In modern English, with notes and introduction, by Professor W. W. SKEAT, Litt.D. Frontispiece, "Ariadne Deserted," after the painting by ANGELICA KAUFMANN.

42. SWIFT'S BATTLE OF THE BOOKS. Together with Selections from the Literature of the Ancient and Modern Learning Controversy.
Edited by A. GUTHKELCH, with notes and introduction. Frontispiece after an old engraving illustrating the Epistles of Phalaris.

43. SIR WILLIAM TEMPLE UPON THE GARDENS OF EPICURUS; together with other XVIIth Century Garden Essays.
Edited, and with notes and introduction, by A. FORBES SIEVEKING, F.S.A. Frontispiece, Portrait of Sir William Temple, and five reproductions of early "Garden" engravings.

44. THE FOUR LAST THINGS, by SIR T. MORE, together with A Spiritual Consolation and other Treatises by JOHN FISHER, Bishop of Rochester.
Edited by DANIEL O'CONNOR. Frontispiece after two designs from the "Daunce of Death." [*In preparation.*]

45. THE SONG OF ROLAND.
Newly translated from the old French by Mrs. CROSLAND. Introduction by Professor BRANDIN, University of London. Frontispiece after a page of the Oxford MS.

THE KING'S CLASSICS

46. DANTE'S VITA NUOVA.
The Italian text with D. G. Rossetti's translation on the opposite page. Introduction and notes by Professor H. Oelsner, Ph.D., Lecturer in Romance Literature, Oxford University. Frontispiece after the original water-colour sketch for "Dante's Dream," by D. G. Rossetti.

47. CHAUCER'S PROLOGUE AND MINOR POEMS.
In modern English by Professor Skeat, Litt.D. Frontispiece, Portrait of Chaucer after the Ellesmere MS.

48. CHAUCER'S PARLIAMENT OF BIRDS AND HOUSE OF FAME.
In modern English by Professor Skeat, Litt.D. Frontispiece, after Sir E. Burne Jones, from the Kelmscott Chaucer.

49. MRS. GASKELL'S CRANFORD.
With an Introduction by R. Brimley Johnson. The frontispiece reproduced after the portrait by Sir W. Richmond, R.A.

50. PEARL.
An English Poem of the Fourteenth Century. Edited with a modern rendering and Introduction by Professor I. Gollancz, Litt.D. With a Frontispiece after W. Holman Hunt, and Prefatory lines by the late Lord Tennyson. A revision of the edition of 1891. (See No. 18.) [*In preparation.*

51, 52. KINGS' LETTERS.
Parts III and IV. Edited from the originals by Robert Steele, F.S.A. (See Nos. 6, 7.) [*In preparation.*

53. THE ENGLISH CORRESPONDENCE OF SAINT BONIFACE.
Being the letters exchanged between "The Apostle of the Germans," while engaged in his missionary labours on the Continent, and his English friends. Translated and edited, and with a brief Introductory sketch of the Life of Saint Boniface, by E. J. Kylie, M.A. [*In preparation.*

THE KING'S CLASSICS 15

54, 55. THE ESSAYS OF ELIA.
Fully edited, with Notes, Introduction, etc., by THOMAS SECCOMBE, M.A. Frontispieces. [*In preparation.*

56. THE CAVALIER TO HIS LADY: an Anthology of XVIIth Century Love Songs.
Selected and edited by FRANK SIDGWICK. With a frontispiece after a water-colour drawing by BYAM SHAW, R.I. [*At Press.*

57. ASSER'S LIFE OF KING ALFRED.
Newly translated and edited by L. C. JANE, M.A. The frontispiece reproduces King Alfred's jewel, while a facsimile is also given of a page of the lost MS.

58. TRANSLATIONS FROM THE ICE-LANDIC: select passages from Icelandic Literature, in prose and verse.
Translated and edited by the Rev. W. C. GREEN, M.A. Frontispiece, a drawing of the Thor Cross, Kirkbride.

59. THE RULE OF ST. BENET.
Translated and edited by the Right Rev. Abbot GASQUET. Frontispiece. [*At Press.*

60. DANIEL'S "DELIA" AND DRAYTON'S "IDEA": two Elizabethan sonnet-sequences.
Edited by ARUNDELL ESDAILE, M.A. Frontispiece, portraits of Daniel and Drayton.

Other volumes in preparation.

NOTE.—*At the date of this list, September* 1908, *Nos.* 1–43, 45–49, 57, 58 *and* 60 *were published. Other numbers subsequent to* 43 *were at press or about to go to press.*

CHATTO & WINDUS, 111 ST. MARTIN'S LANE, LONDON, W.C.

THE SHAKESPEARE LIBRARY

General Editor, Professor I. Gollancz, Litt.D.

Part I. THE OLD-SPELLING SHAKESPEARE, in 40 Vols. Edited by Dr. F. J. Furnivall, with the assistance of F. W. Clarke, M.A. In the case of several volumes the late W. G. Boswell-Stone rendered invaluable assistance before his death.

Part II. THE SHAKESPEARE CLASSICS: a series of reprints embodying the Novels, Plays and Romances, used by Shakespeare as the originals or direct sources of his Plays.

Part III. THE LAMB SHAKESPEARE FOR THE YOUNG: edited by Prof. Gollancz. Each volume is illustrated and contains the chief songs set to music for home or school use under the direction of T. Maskell Hardy.

Part IV. SHAKESPEARE'S ENGLAND: a series of volumes illustrative of the life, thought, and letters of England in Shakespeare's time.

The detailed prospectus post free on application.

BIBLIOTHECA ROMANICA

Under the sub-headings—*Bibliothèque Française, Biblioteca Italiana, Biblioteca Española, Biblioteca Portuguesa*—are here issued selected classics of the Romance Languages, in, and with notes and necessary introductions also in the original language of the several volumes. Cartridge paper binding 8*d.* net, cloth 1*s.* net. Fifty-seven Volumes are now ready, and others will follow.

The detailed prospectus post free on application.

Chatto & Windus Publishers	111 St. Martin's Lane, London, W.C.

[*R. Clay & Sons, Ltd., London and Bungay.*

BIBLIOLIFE

Old Books Deserve a New Life
www.bibliolife.com

Did you know that you can get most of our titles in our trademark **EasyScript**™ print format? **EasyScript**™ provides readers with a larger than average typeface, for a reading experience that's easier on the eyes.

Did you know that we have an ever-growing collection of books in many languages?

Order online:
www.bibliolife.com/store

Or to exclusively browse our **EasyScript**™ collection:
www.bibliogrande.com

At BiblioLife, we aim to make knowledge more accessible by making thousands of titles available to you – quickly and affordably.

Contact us:
BiblioLife
PO Box 21206
Charleston, SC 29413

Printed in Great Britain
by Amazon.co.uk, Ltd.,
Marston Gate.